Grammar of
the Shot

Grammar of the Shot

SECOND EDITION

Roy Thompson

Christopher J. Bowen

AMSTERDAM • BOSTON • HEIDELBERG • LONDON
NEW YORK • OXFORD • PARIS • SAN DIEGO
SAN FRANCISCO • SINGAPORE • SYDNEY • TOKYO
Focal Press is an imprint of Elsevier

Focal Press is an imprint of Elsevier
30 Corporate Drive, Suite 400, Burlington, MA 01803, USA
Linacre House, Jordan Hill, Oxford OX2 8DP, UK

Library of Congress Cataloging-in-Publication Data
Application submitted

British Library Cataloguing-in-Publication Data
A catalogue record for this book is available from the British Library.

ISBN: 978-0-240-52121-3

For information on all Focal Press publications
visit our website at www.elsevierdirect.com

09 10 11 12 5 4 3 2 1

Printed in the United States of America

Working together to grow
libraries in developing countries

www.elsevier.com | www.bookaid.org | www.sabre.org

ELSEVIER   BOOK AID
              International   Sabre Foundation

Contents

Acknowledgments   ix

Introduction   xi

Chapter One – The Shot and How to Frame It   1
  What to Show Your Audience?   4
  Aspect Ratio   6
  The Basic Building Blocks—The Different Shot Type Families   8
    Medium Shot   8
    Close-Up   8
    Long Shot   10
  The Extended Family of Basic Shots   12
    Extreme Long Shot   12
    Very Long Shot   14
    Long Shot/Wide Shot   14
    Medium Long Shot   15
    Medium Shot   16
    Medium Close-Up   17
    Close-Up   17
    Big Close-Up   19
    Extreme Close-Up   19
  End of Chapter One Review   21

Chapter Two – The Art of Composition   23
  Simple Rules for Framing Human Subjects   24
  Headroom   25
  Subjective vs Objective Shooting Styles   26
  Look Room   28
  The Rule of Thirds   30
  Camera Angle   32
  Horizontal Camera Angles   34
  Vertical Camera Angles   40
  High Angle Shot   41
  Low Angle Shot   42
  The Two-Shot: Frame Composition with Two People   44

The Profile Two-Shot   45
The Direct to Camera Two-Shot   48
The Over-the-Shoulder Two-Shot   50
Wrapping up the Basics of Composition   52
End of Chapter Two Review   52

Chapter Three – Composition—Beyond the Basics   53
The Third Dimension   54
The Horizon Line   56
Dutch Angle   59
Diagonal Lines   60
The Depth of Film Space—Foreground/Middle Ground/Background   63
    Foreground   63
    Middle Ground   64
    Background   64
Depth Cues   65
The Camera Lens—The Eye in Composition   66
The Zoom Lens   66
Lens Focus—Directing the Viewer's Eye Around Your Frame   70
    Pulling Focus vs Following Focus   71
Light in Composition—Now You See It, Now You Don't   74
Light as Energy   76
Color Temperature   77
Natural or Artificial Light   78
Quantity of Light: Sensitivity and Exposure   80
Quality of Light: Hard vs Soft   82
Contrast   84
Basic Character Lighting: Three Point Method   86
Set and Location Lighting   90
End of Chapter Three Review   92

Chapter Four – Putting Your Shots Together: Prethinking the Editing Process   93
Matching Your Shots in a Scene   95
Continuity   96
Continuity of Screen Direction   97
The Line—Basis for Screen Direction   100
The Imaginary Line—The 180 Degree Rule   102
"Jumping the Line"   104

The 30 Degree Rule   106

Reciprocating Imagery   108

Eye-Line Match   111

End of Chapter Four Review   112

Chapter Five – Dynamic Shots—Talent and Camera in Motion   **113**

Blocking Talent   114

Camera in Motion   115

Handheld   116

   Advantages   116

   Disadvantages   116

Pan and Tilt   117

Shooting the Pan and the Tilt   120

   The Start Frame   120

   The Camera Movement   120

   The End Frame   120

Equipment Used to Move the Camera   122

Tripod   123

Dolly   124

Crab   126

Truck   127

   Steadicam   128

Cranes and Such   129

End of Chapter Five Review   130

Chapter Six – Working Practices and General Guidelines   **131**

Communicating with Talent   132

Shooting a Big Close-Up or Extreme Close-Up   134

Ensure an Eye Light   136

Safe Action Line and Domestic Cutoff   138

Follow Action with Loose Pan and Tilt Tripod Head   139

Shooting Overlapping Action for the Edit   140

   Continuity of Action   140

   Matching Speed of Action   140

   Overlapping Too Much Action   141

Shooting Ratio   142

Storyboards and Shot Lists   143

Always Have Something in Focus   144

Frame for Correct "Look Room" on Shots That Will Edit Together   146

Shoot Matching Camera Angles When Covering Dialogue 148

Place Important Objects in the Top Half of Your Frame 150

Be Aware of the Color Choices Made Throughout Your Project 151

Always Be Aware of Headroom 152

Keep Distracting Objects Out of the Shot 153

Use the Depth of Your Film Space to Stage Shots with Several People 154

In a Three Person Dialogue Scene, Matching Two Shots Can Be
Problematic for the Editor 155

Try to Always Show Both Eyes of Your Subject 156

Be Aware of Eye-Line Directions in Closer Shots 158

Understand When and How to Perform a Zoom during a Shot 160

Motivate Your Truck In and Truck Out Dolly Moves 162

Ways to Cross the 180 Degree Line Safely 163

Allow the Camera More Time to Record Each Shot 165

Allow All Actions to Complete before Cutting Camera 166

During Documentary Shooting Be as Discrete as Possible 167

Beware of Continuity Traps While Shooting a Scene 168

Use Short Focal Length Lenses to Hide Camera Movement 169

Beware of Wide Lenses When Shooting Close-Up Shots 170

Control Your Depth of Field 172

Slate the Head of Your Shots 174

End of Chapter Six Review 176

Chapter Seven – In Conclusion **177**

Know the Rules Before You Break the Rules 178

The Reason for Shooting Is Editing 179

Your Shots Should Enhance the Entire Story 180

Involve the Viewer as Much as Possible 181

Try Hard Not to Be Obtrusive 183

Know Your Equipment 184

Be Familiar with Your Subject 185

Understand Lighting—Both Natural and Artificial 186

Study What Has Already Been Done 187

In Summation 188

Glossary **189**

Index **209**

Acknowledgments

I wish to thank my editors at Focal Press, Elinor Actipis and Michele Cronin, for presenting me with the wonderful opportunity to write the second edition of this time honored text, *Grammar of the Shot*. Of course, this would not be possible without the ground work done by Mr. Roy Thompson on the first edition. I hope that this revised version continues to inform and inspire all those readers who are just beginning their creative journey into the world of shooting motion pictures.

As an educator today, I wish to acknowledge the positive impact that my instructors at Brandeis University and Boston University had on me during my own higher education. The broad scope of the Liberal Arts was great preparation for the specific focus and technical craftsmanship that come with the field of film production. I present these same values to my own students and I thank them collectively for all they brought to me.

As a media professional today, I wish to thank my many colleagues and clients who have helped me to continue learning with each new project undertaken.

I am also grateful for the advice offered by several generous peers in the preparation of this second edition—John Caro, Robert J. de Maria, Robert Harris, Michael Kowalski, and Michael Lawler.

Additionally, I would like to thank my on-camera talent for their time on this project— Wendy Chao, Hannah Kurth, Alexander Scott, Stacy Shreffler, and Eliza Smith. All photographs are by the author as are the line art diagrams and many of the illustrations. I must offer my thanks and appreciation to my co-illustrator, Jean Sharpe, whose distinct style and generous contributions make this text a better learning tool. Also, I offer a note of kind thanks to Mary James for her advice and assistance.

Lastly, I acknowledge my family for their support and offer extra special thanks to Rachael Swain who has been there through the thick and thin of it all and really helped pull all the pieces together.

This book is for all people who wish to learn the basics about shooting film and video. I hope you have fun and enjoy the ride. If you would like to learn more about the topic, find additional resources, or learn more about the author, please visit the author's website www.fellswaycreatives.com.

Introduction

One gets the impression that life today is all about experiencing communication in one form or another. We are constantly speaking on mobile telephones, watching television, using the Internet, listening to the radio, reading books, newspapers and magazines, looking at billboards and advertisements, going to the movies, and so forth. Our ability to understand these communications and gain further meaning from them is reliant upon our education—can we read, write and speak a language, recognize images and sounds, decipher symbols, etc.

This education, whether it is from schooling or just living life, helps determine how well we can compute what we take in. Collectively, over time, we have learned to codify our visual communications—from pictographs, to written words, to paintings, photographs and now motion pictures. What we depict has a recognizable meaning. Viewers know how to decode the images that they are shown. Understanding, or clear interpretation of what is viewed, stems from the established grammar or rules of depiction that have evolved over time.

It is this concept of grammar—meaning gleaned from structure—which motion picture creators rely upon so heavily. Fictional narrative films, documentaries, news reports, situation comedies, television dramas, commercials, music videos, talk shows, "reality" programming, and the like, all use the same basic visual grammar to help communicate to the viewer. As a filmmaker, when you "speak" the common film language, you will be able to communicate your story to a global audience.

This text, *Grammar of the Shot*, is designed for those of you who are new to the realm of visual storytelling but who wish to be well acquainted with the basic rules, conventions, and practices of the global visual language of motion pictures. It will take you from the basic shape of the frame, to the different types of shots, to the ways to compose visual elements within those frames. You will be exposed to the basics of shot lighting, screen direction, 3D elements, camera movement and many general practices that make for a richer, multi-layered visual presentation. Most importantly, it will provide you with essential information to expand your visual vocabulary and help jumpstart your motion imaging career in this ever-evolving world of visual communications.

Chapter One
The Shot and How to Frame It

QUESTION: What is a shot?

ANSWER: A shot is the smallest unit of visual information captured at one time by the camera that shows a certain action or event.

So you want to shoot a feature film, a funny short for the web, or candid interviews for your cousin's wedding video, but you are not quite sure how to go about it? Well, this book will be a good place for you to start learning. And just as you learned in school how to properly read and write your primary spoken language, you will have to become familiar with the standard and accepted rules of motion picture visual language. Unlike the many complex and seemingly contradictory rules of grammar for spoken languages around the world, the grammar of the shot, or film language, is the same for all cultures of the globe. It is a common language. It is a globally accepted way of depicting people, things, and actions such that they become instantly understood by all who perceive the images.

If we are going to be discussing the grammar of the shot, then we are going to have to define what we mean by grammar and what we mean by shot. Well it should be understood that grammar in this sense of the word refers to the basic rules governing the construction and presentation of visual elements that are created for inclusion in a motion picture. These are the commonly accepted guidelines that define how visual information should be displayed to a viewer. Viewers, all of us who have grown up watching films and television, have been trained over the years to observe, decode, and comprehend the various elements of the various shots used in motion picture creation. In other words, we may not consciously express it, but we know what certain images mean and how they make us feel. An adept filmmaker uses this dynamic between the shots and the viewer to tell better stories.

A shot is the recording of one action from one particular point of view at one time. Even though the action may be repeated several times (or **takes**) from that same angle or camera position in order to get it right, as with fictional narrative shooting, it is still that one shot. If you were to change the **camera angle**, camera position, or lens **focal length** (all covered in more detail throughout the book) then the result of that recorded image would be a different shot—a different way of viewing the action—even if the exact same action from a previous **camera setup** is repeated and captured. Each shot, when originally recorded, will be unique.

So we will explore what the basic types of shots are and what goes into their creation. We will also see what information and meaning can be pulled out of these shots by the viewer. Remember, filmmaking is simultaneously a creative and technical craft, and the extent of your success often depends upon how well you communicate your vision to your audience. It is an audience who must consume, digest, and understand your pictures; if you confuse them with bad film language or improper visual "grammar" then they will most likely not respond well to your work.

In order to keep things simple, we are, for the most part, going to try and use generic terms for discussion and explanation. For instance, the term "motion picture" will be used to represent any work, show, project, or program that is made up of individual images that, when displayed to our eyes very rapidly, appear to move. The term camera will refer to any device that can record these moving images—whether it is emulsion film, video tape, or direct to hard drive. The terms **camera person** or **camera operator** will refer to anyone, man or woman, who operates the camera that is recording the moving images.

What to Show Your Audience?

Since movies and television shows rely so heavily on their visual elements, you have to decide very early on in the creation process what is important for the viewer to see and how they should be shown that information, action, event, or detail. This choice of what to actually photograph can be the result of input from many people involved in the project—from the writer to the director to the **director of photography** to the actor to a producer. Regardless of who makes the choice, someone will, and for your initial projects it will most likely be you.

The script of a fictional narrative story or the real-time events of a documentary will help guide the choices of what to actually frame up and capture with the camera and the lens. The camera and the lens work together to record a particular horizontal rectangle of reality. That rectangle is only a small segment or cutout window of the total sphere of the physical world around the camera operator. This cutout has a defined and finite border, called the **frame** (see Figure 1.1). Whatever is inside this frame is recorded as a two-dimensional (2D) representation of the actual world before the lens. At present, because our film and video cameras can really only capture the two dimensions of width and height (frame left to right and frame top to bottom), they get displayed as flat images on a projected movie screen, television screen, or computer screen. The third dimension, depth, although present in the reality before the camera, is only captured as an illusion of depth on the actual 2D film or video. This concept is discussed in more detail in Chapter 2.

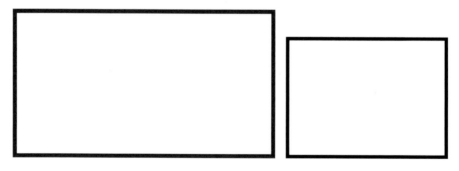

FIGURE 1.1   Basic widescreen 16 × 9 frame and basic standard definition 4 × 3 television frame. Think of these as your empty canvases where you will get to "paint" the various elements of your shots.

Not to get too technical at the outset, but this next topic, frame size and **aspect ratio**, really should be addressed early on so that you can begin shooting your project with a solid understanding of the visual frame. It is the camera's format (the area of width and height of the imager) and the type of lens used that really dictate what you ultimately record and what the audience may ultimately watch within the 2D rectangular frame of motion that you capture. We will discuss lenses later, but we should address this topic of frame sizes now, since it is your choice of camera (**Video Format** or **Film Gauge** with variable masking) that determines the shape and size of the final frame.

What to Show Your Audience?

Aspect Ratio

The dimensions of a camera's frame (the active recordable image area) or the width-to-height relationship of that frame is often expressed as a ratio of that width to that height. This ratio is called the aspect ratio and, depending on the format of the medium, may be written 4:3, 16:9, 1.85:1, and so on. The first example, 4:3 (said "four to three" and sometimes "four by three"), means that if the height is three units tall, then the width is equal to four of those same units. This is the aspect ratio for **standard definition** (SD) television in North America (NTSC and NTSC miniDV) and Europe (PAL, and DV-PAL). It can also be represented by the ratio of 1.33:1 (which is said "one-three-three to one"), where the number "1" represents the standard frame height and the number "1.33" shows that the width of the frame is 1.33 times as long as the height. All **high definition** (HD) video is 16:9 (which is said "sixteen to nine" and often written 16 × 9, or "sixteen by nine"), meaning a wide screen aspect ratio where there is a unit of measure 16 across and only 9 of those same units tall.

Figure 1.2 shows several of these frame sizes or aspect ratios from television and motion picture history. The size has evolved over the decades as technologies changed. At present, theatrical motion pictures, standard definition, and high definition television all have different aspect ratios, and it makes it rather confusing and complicated to make the images of one

FIGURE 1.2   Comparison of various frame sizes from the history of film and video. Note the tendency to move toward a wider frame.

format fit into the shape of another, but we will not worry about that now. We will simply select a single frame size and work with that. The global movement toward widescreen digital HDTV (16:9) is undeniable so we are going to use the 16:9 aspect ratio for our examples. If you are using any gauge of film, NTSC-DV or PAL-DV, you have nothing to fear—our examples will all translate into your rectangular frame shape. The beauty of film language is that no matter what aspect ratio you frame and shoot, the rules of the grammar remain unchanged, as they have remained relatively unchanged for the past nine decades or so.

Further Exploration—A Brief History of Aspect Ratios

Theatrical motion pictures in North America have been widescreen (1.85:1) for a long time now. European widescreen theatres projected 1.66:1 images. Standard definition television sets at home (roughly 1.33:1) have been less rectangular than widescreen—until recently with the advent of HDTV (roughly 1.78:1 or 16 × 9). There are several reasons for these differences, but the gist of it is that classical Hollywood 35-mm motion picture film had, for many years, used an aspect ratio of 1.33:1 (more square-like than rectangular). When television became popular, the broadcasters needed material to play, and Hollywood could offer up several decades of motion pictures to be displayed—thus the 1.33:1 television aspect ratio.

As television became more popular, and in order to compete with that popularity, the movie industry began to create widescreen aspect ratio film formats such as VistaVision, Cinemascope, and so on. Thus, the more modern widescreen aspect ratio was born. The problem has been that 1.33:1 television has been too small a frame size to show the wider 1.85:1, 1.66:1, and certainly the 2.4:1 movies. A process called pan and scan was developed so that the smaller screen could extract its view from the larger, wider original film's aspect ratio to show the television audience. What gets cut off, however, was always intended to be seen but now it is lost. As HDTV (the newer 16 × 9 television set) enters into more and more homes, its native widescreen aspect ratio more closely matches the widescreen of the feature films and there is not as much need for this "cutting off" of the original frame. It can be argued that the wider screen, that longer, more horizontally rectangular shape, is better for image capture—its shape appeals to our eyes more because the field of view (what we get to watch) is closer to what our eyes see naturally when we look at the world. So let us explore the grammar of the shot based on this new, wider 16 × 9 framing.

Aspect Ratio

The Basic Building Blocks—The Different Shot Type Families

We know that a **shot** is the smallest unit of photographic coverage of a person, action, or event in a motion picture. We also know, from watching movies and television programming, that the persons, actions, and events we see are not all shown from the same exact angle, perspective, or distance. Therefore, although each shot represents a unique way to cover or frame the action, it is clear that there are a variety of common **shot types**. Perhaps the terms close-up, medium shot, and long shot are already familiar to you, but let us take a look at an example of each shot type. Keep in mind, we are going to first explore the simplest of shots (static, **locked-off** shots) of a person (the subject within the frame) and then build in complexity of content and composition. So let us begin at the beginning.

Medium Shot

The medium shot (also abbreviated MS) is the shot type that nearly approximates how we, as humans, see the environment most immediately around us. Imagine that you are in a room with another person and the two of you are engaged in conversation. Typically there would be several feet of space between you (unless you were particularly close friends or the room was extraordinarily tiny) and, as a result, you would most likely be viewing each other in a medium shot. Then imagine that you are holding a camera and you record the other person's image. The resulting frame would most likely yield what is known as a medium shot. So it would seem that proximity or distance from the observer (you or the camera) can help dictate what is seen in the frame. A moderate distance then (let us say 5 to 10 feet) may lead to a medium shot. We will explore other factors, such as actual object size and focal length of lens on the camera, later in the text. What it really comes down to, though, is how much of a person, object, or environment is included in the frame. A viewer watching a medium shot should feel very comfortable with the image because it should feel like a normal observation (see Figure 1.3).

Close-Up

The close-up (CU) is the intimate shot. It provides a magnified view of some person, object, or action. As a result, it can yield rather specific, detailed information to the viewer. If we continue the example from earlier, imagine that person with whom you are having the conversation in that room holds a picture of their new car. In that medium

FIGURE 1.3 A medium shot with a single human subject.

FIGURE 1.4 A close-up with a single human subject.

shot, you would most likely only be able to see that it is a photograph, but certain details would be lacking. Then, if you take that photograph and hold it closer to your eyes you would see it much better. You just created a close-up of the photograph so that you could observe more detail and get more precise information—you clearly see the photograph of a new car. Again, object size, proximity, and magnification (lens optics at play) will help you generate this frame filled with a larger rendering of the object (see Figure 1.4).

The Basic Building Blocks—The Different Shot Type Families

FIGURE 1.5   A long shot with a single human subject.

Long Shot

The long shot (LS) is a more inclusive shot. It frames much more of the environment around the person, object, or action and often shows their relationships in physical space much better. As a result, the environment may take up much more of the screen than the person or the object included in the frame. To continue our example, the person who just showed you the photograph of their new car gestures toward the window and tells you to look outside at the actual car parked out on the street. When you view the car from the window, you are seeing it in a long shot. The car is far away, small in your frame of view, and surrounded by more information from the entire environment. The long shot may also be referred to as the wide shot (WS) because it traditionally encompasses more of the filmed world within its frame. A viewer is presented a wider field of visual information, often shot from a long distance away (see Figure 1.5).

These three major types of shots—MS, CU, and LS—will be the basic building blocks that you will use to start capturing your moving imagery. It will be up to you, the film-maker/camera person, which shot type you use to cover the various persons, objects, or actions in your visual story. To help you decide, you may find it useful to ask yourself,

"If I were watching this motion picture, what would I want to be seeing right now?" Remember, it is the audience who ultimately watches all of your shots edited together, and their experience viewing your piece is based, in large part, upon the quality and variety of shot types that you can present to them. Next, we will elaborate much more on the other, numerous derivations of these three basic shots. So do not worry, you will have plenty of shot variety to cover all of the action.

The Basic Building Blocks—The Different Shot Type Families

The Extended Family of Basic Shots

Basic shots represent the most straight forward depiction of a human subject. The illustrative examples presented here are an introduction to the various magnitudes of shots that you will be able to create in each category. In order to keep things as simple as possible, the illustrations will assume a single subject in a plain environment with the recording camera placed roughly at the same height as the subject's eyes (this camera placement is a relatively standard way of shooting a person from a neutral position). For now we will maintain a character stance central in the frame, and looking straight to lens. This basic presentation is just for training purposes, you will later understand more numerous and much better ways to compose the images.

The following is a list of the basic shots (Figure 1.6):

- Extreme long shot
- Very long shot
- Long shot/wide shot
- Medium long shot
- Medium shot
- Medium close-up
- Close-up
- Big close-up
- Extreme close-up

Extreme Long Shot

1. May be abbreviated as either XLS or ELS
2. Also referred to as a very wide shot or a very wide angle shot
3. Traditionally used in **exterior** shooting
4. Encompasses a large field of view, therefore forms an image that shows a large amount of the environment within the **film space**
5. Often used as an **establishing shot** at the beginning of a motion picture or at the start of a new sequence within a motion picture
6. Shows where—urban, suburban, rural, mountains, desert, ocean, etc.
7. May show when—day, night, summer, winter, spring, fall, distant past, past, present, future, etc.

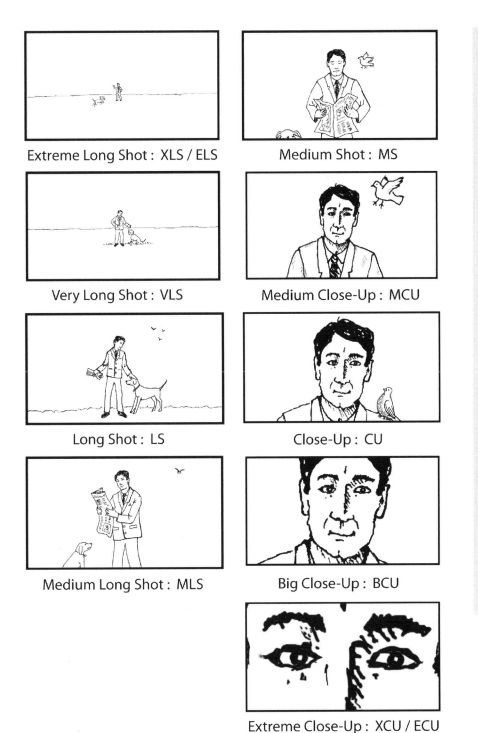

Extreme Long Shot : XLS / ELS

Medium Shot : MS

Very Long Shot : VLS

Medium Close-Up : MCU

Long Shot : LS

Close-Up : CU

Medium Long Shot : MLS

Big Close-Up : BCU

Extreme Close-Up : XCU / ECU

The Extended Family of Basic Shots

FIGURE 1.6 Examples of the nine shot types.

FIGURE 1.7 Example of an XLS.

8. May show who—lone stranger walking into town, massive invading army—most often the human figures in the XLS are so small that details are not distinguishable—general, not specific, information will be conveyed (Figure 1.7)

Very Long Shot

1. May be abbreviated VLS
2. Also in the wide shot family
3. May be used in exterior or **interior** shooting when enough width and height exist within the studio set or location building, such as an open warehouse
4. Environment within the film space is still very important as it fills much of the screen, but the human figure is more visible and clothing detail may be observed
5. May be used as an establishing shot where movement of character brings the figure closer to the camera
6. Shows where, when, and a bit more of who (Figure 1.8)

Long Shot/Wide Shot

1. Abbreviated LS and/or WS
2. This is usually considered a "full body" shot, wide but in close to a figure with head and feet visible in the frame
3. Interior or exterior shooting
4. Larger human figure takes attention away from the environment; however, a fair amount of the character's surroundings is still visible

FIGURE 1.8 Example of a VLS.

FIGURE 1.9 Example of a long shot.

5. May not work well for an establishing shot
6. Shows where, when and who—the gender, clothing, movements, and general facial expressions may be observed more easily (Figure 1.9)

Medium Long Shot

1. Abbreviated MLS
2. First shot in increasing magnitude that cuts off a body part of the subject— traditionally framed such that bottom of frame cuts off the leg either just below or, more commonly, just above the knee. The choice for where to cut may depend on costuming or body movement of the individual in the shot. If you cut off above

FIGURE 1.10 Example of a medium long shot.

the knee, it is sometimes referred to as the "Cowboy" because in American Western movies there was interest in being able to show the firearm in the holster strapped to the thigh of a cowboy.

3. May be interior or exterior shot
4. Human figure is prominent; details in clothing, gender, and facial expressions are visible
5. Shows more of who than where and may still show when (Figure 1.10)

Medium Shot

1. Abbreviated MS
2. May also be called the "Waist" shot, as the frame cuts off the human figure just below the waist and just above the wrist if arms are down at the side.
3. Interior or exterior
4. Human figure is most prominent in the frame—eyes and the direction they look, clothing, hair color, and style are all plainly visible
5. Subject movement may become a concern, as the tighter framing restricts the freedom of gesture—be careful not to **break frame** (have an actor's body part touch or move beyond the established edge of the picture frame)
6. Certainly shows who and may provide generic detail about where (inside or outside, apartment, store, forest, etc.) and when (day or night, season) (Figure 1.11)

FIGURE 1.11   Example of a medium shot.

Medium Close-Up

1. Abbreviated MCU
2. Sometimes called a "two-button" for the tight bottom frame cutting off at the chest, roughly where you would see the top two buttons on a shirt. Definitely cuts off above the elbow joint. Adjust bottom frame slightly for men or women depending on costuming
3. Interior or exterior
4. Character's facial features are rather clear—where the eyes look is obvious, as is emotion, hair style and color, make-up, etc. This is one of the most commonly used shots in filmmaking because it provides so much information about the character while speaking, listening, or performing an action that does not involve much body or head movement
5. An audience is supposed to be watching the human face at this point in the framing so actions or objects in the surrounding environment hold little to no importance
6. Depending on general lighting and costuming, you may discern general information about where and when (Figure 1.12)

Close-Up

1. Abbreviated CU
2. Sometimes called a "head shot," as the framing may cut off the top of the subject's hair and the bottom of the frame can begin anywhere just below the chin or with a little upper shoulder visible (costuming and hairstyle dependent)

FIGURE 1.12 Example of a medium close-up.

FIGURE 1.13 Example of a close-up.

3. Interior or exterior
4. A very intimate full face shot of a human subject showing all detail in the eyes and conveys the subtle emotions that play across the eyes, mouth, and facial muscles of an actor—health conditions and facial hair in men and make-up use in women are clearly visible
5. An audience member should be totally focused on the human face with this framing, especially the eyes and/or mouth
6. Who but not so much where or when (Figure 1.13)

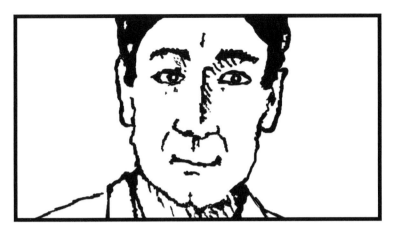

FIGURE 1.14   Example of big close-up.

Big Close-Up

1. Abbreviated BCU
2. Human face occupies as much of the frame as possible and still shows the key features of eyes, nose, and mouth at once
3. Interior or exterior
4. Such an intimate shot puts the audience directly in the face of the subject— because every detail of the face is highly visible, facial movements or expressions need to be subtle—very little head movement can be tolerated before the subject moves out of frame
5. This shot is about who and how that "who" feels—angry, scared, romantic, etc. (Figure 1.14)

Extreme Close-Up

1. Abbreviated ECU or XCU
2. Purely a detail shot—framing favors one aspect of a subject such as his/her eyes, mouth, ear, or hand
3. Lacking any points of reference to the surrounding environment, the audience has no context in which to place this body part detail, so understanding will stem from how or when this shot is edited into the motion picture—it may be helpful if the subject whose body detail is displayed in the XCU is first shown in a wider shot so context may be established for the viewer

The Extended Family of Basic Shots

FIGURE 1.15   Example of an extreme close-up.

4. This type of extremely magnified imagery can be used in documentary work, such as medical films or scientific studies, and may be used in fictional narrative, although sparingly, and experimental art films (Figure 1.15)

End of Chapter One Review

1. Visual "grammar" or film language is understood around the world.

2. The format of your camera initially determines the shape of your frame.

3. The aspect ratio describes the dimensions of your active recording area.

4. The three basic shot types are the medium shot, close-up, and long shot.

5. The extended family of nine shot types ranges from extreme long shot to extreme close-up.

Chapter Two
The Art of Composition

QUESTION: What is composition?

ANSWER: Put simply, composition is the unified arrangement of artistic parts inherent to the "art form" being practiced. One can compose music, steps in a dance routine, figures in a painting, words on a page, visual elements within a film frame, and so forth.

Since you now understand that a shot pictorially covers a person, action, or event within a certain frame size, we have to take a more refined look at how you could fill that frame with the important objects, or the important "information." Meaning, where, specifically, do you place the person's head in a close-up shot or where, specifically, do you place that lone, tall tree on the flat ranch land in a long shot? And it is not only where you place them but why. The arrangement of these visual elements and their placement within the overall frame is very important and will convey particular meanings to the audience. This is the power of picture composition and we will explore ways to compose shots and what those compositions might mean to the "message" behind the grammar of the shots.

Again, you get to decide what you capture on your motion picture frame, so let us go ahead and place a camera in your hands. Okay. Now what? Well, first you will have to understand what that camera's format is and what it has for a frame aspect ratio. Knowing the exact shape of the frame, you now understand the boundaries of width and height that are going to help you decide the other various shooting options ahead of you. Next, decide what you would like to shoot in the world around you, point the camera at something, and record the images. A new creative decision arises here—you know the object(s) to be captured, but you have to be equally aware of how you place the object(s) within the frame. It is this artful placement of objects about the frame that helps underscore meaning, provides subtext, and, in general, imbues your imagery with an internal sense of beauty, balance, and order. This is the art of composition.

Simple Rules for Framing Human Subjects

Let us try to start with something simple that you will have to shoot many, many times: a medium close-up of a human face. We shall see that what at first seems rather simple will, in fact, require you to make many creative choices—choices that will help make your images better, stronger, and more understandable in the long run.

Here is a medium close-up (Figure 2.1).

FIGURE 2.1   Generic medium close-up.

What do you notice about this image? Where is the person's head located within the frame? Where do the person's eyes look? The head is very close to center frame and the eyes are looking directly into the lens—straight at you, the audience member. Let us handle the head placement first.

Headroom

Within a given shot type (MS, LS, CU) there is a generally accepted guideline as to where the head of a person should be placed within the frame. This guideline applies much more to MS and CU shots because in these tighter shots you mostly see the person's body and head and much less of the environment. Human beings naturally tend to look each other in the face and, specifically, in the eyes when communicating. This "face focus" allows us to gain insight into the physical and mental health of an individual and to get a handle on their emotional state. Therefore, when an audience member watches an actor on screen they will most often look at the person's face, particularly at the eyes and the mouth. Filmmakers know this to be true and they count on it when composing an individual's shot.

The placement of the head within the frame is very important, which is why we have the guideline of **headroom**. Headroom specifically refers to how much or how little space exists between the top of an actor's head and the top edge of the recorded frame. Because screen space is at a premium, it would be a shame to waste it, so we often set the top of the frame to cut off just above the talent's head in a tighter shot. In wider shots you should also consider how much screen space above the talent you allow to exist. Unless the story or event calls for some extra room above the head, you let it go in favor of more information at midframe. Later, when we review examples of closer shots, you will see how it is appropriate to also cut off the hair and tops of people's heads as long as you keep their eyes and mouths well framed within the screen space. So, in general, try not to give too much headroom as it wastes screen space and can throw off the overall composition (Figure 2.2).

FIGURE 2.2 Medium close-up with adjusted headroom.

Headroom

Subjective vs Objective Shooting Styles

Now let us address how the person's eyes are looking straight at us. What might it mean if the person being recorded by the camera looks directly into the lens? How does it make you, the viewer, feel when you are addressed directly by on-screen talent? Of course, it may depend on the kind of project you are shooting or watching. If you are photographing a news reporter on location then it would make sense for the on-camera talent to look straight into the camera's lens and deliver the factual report. The reporter makes a direct connection with you, the home audience, by looking you square in the eye and speaking the truth. Maybe you shoot a talk show host or footage for a do-it-yourself home makeover show with a crazy host—whoever it is, these television programming genres have an accepted rule that a person may look directly into the lens and address the viewer. Many call this style of camera work **subjective shooting**.

This is not so for scripted fictional narrative projects (at least for the most part—as you will grow to learn, there are often exceptions to the rules). With a fictional story you have actors playing roles in a pretend world. The camera is almost always an observer, not a direct participant. The talent is not supposed to look directly into the lens—and often, not even near it. If an actor looks into the lens, or addresses the camera, it is called "**breaking the fourth wall**." If the camera were in a room recording the actions of a performer, the camera may see the back wall and the two side walls. The wall behind the camera, that is, the wall that should be physically in place where the camera is positioned, is the "fourth wall." It is the place from where the actions are being recorded and, ultimately, the place where the viewing audience is privileged to sit and observe the story. All on-screen talent behave as though the camera is not even there. This style of camera work is often called **objective shooting**.

For ease of demonstration, let us continue our medium close-up examples as though we are shooting for a fictional narrative film project where an objective shooting style is the goal. So let us take our subject's eyes off the axis of the lens (Figure 2.3).

This is a good start, but the face is still front on. This can cause a flattening to the facial features and is not always that flattering to talent or that interesting for the viewer. Let us put a small shift on how the talent is standing in relation to the camera (Figure 2.4).

FIGURE 2.3 MCU of talent with eyes looking away from lens axis.

FIGURE 2.4 Talent turns body and eyes off lens axis by one-fourth turn.

Look Room

Our composition of this individual is getting better, but the center framing is not working so well. Notice how the face in the center of the screen is looking off to the side—at someone or something yet to be shown in another shot. A centralized framing like this is very solid but perhaps it is too uniform, too symmetrical, or too compositionally boring. Let us create more **look room** (Figure 2.5).

Look room (also called **looking room** or **nose room**) is the empty space that we have provided within the frame, between the talent's eyes and the edge of the frame opposite the face. It is this empty area, or "**negative space**" that helps balance out this new frame where the weight of the object (the talent's head) occupies frame left and the weight of the empty space occupies frame right. In this case, the word "weight" really implies a visual mass whether it is an actual object, such as a head, or an empty space, such as the void filling frame right. We will see later how this negative space and the direction of the actor's gaze impel an audience to also want to see what the actor is looking at, but for now, let us stay focused on where in the frame the head is placed.

FIGURE 2.5   Placing head on frame left allows the talent to look across the empty space.

What if we moved the head to the opposite side of the screen but kept the face and eyes looking in the current direction (Figure 2.6)?

The look room for this framing is severely cut off on frame right and we have a large, empty space on frame left. Our weighted objects—the head and the void—still exist, but their placement just does not feel correct. The actor's face is too close to the near "wall" of the frame, making it look congested, claustrophobic, and trapped. Also, one gets the sense that the empty space occupying the majority of frame left is crying out to be filled with someone or something. That negative space behind the head can imply negative feelings of suspense, dread, vulnerability, and so on and unless that is your creative intention, it would be best to not frame the actor this way.

Our original example MCU with the head at the center of the frame is not wrong, mind you; it is just not always as visually interesting to keep your objects of interest at the center of the frame. That may work well for still photographic portraiture, but it lacks a certain punch for motion picture imagery. You will become quite adept at placing important objects on one side of the frame or the other over time. We will discuss the direction of the look room in more detail later in the text, but right now let us introduce you to another rule or guideline that will help you place these objects within the frame.

Look Room

FIGURE 2.6   No look room creates a void crying out to be filled.

The Rule of Thirds

We moved the actor's head off toward frame left in our MCU example in order to generate a more balanced frame of weighted objects. Notice that we did not choose framing like the examples shown in Figures 2.7 and 2.8.

We could create frames like this for particular reasons, but for the most part we are going to be following the accepted grammar, and the **rule of thirds** is definitely one

FIGURE 2.7   Back of talent's head is too close to frame left, breaking the frame edge.

FIGURE 2.8   Cutting the face in half may be considered "artsy" or "experimental" so beware.

of those points to follow. The rule of thirds is very easy to remember and very simple to execute. Take your frame and divide it up into thirds, both vertically and horizontally (Figure 2.9).

Of course, these lines are never going to physically live on your frame. You have to know their approximate placement on your particular viewfinder in your camera. So, when searching for a rule of thirds composition, you may choose to frame your talent as shown in Figure 2.10.

One can also place visual elements at the crossing points where two of the lines intersect. In this case, the eyes within the head of our MCU figure are placed roughly at this crossing point (see Figure 2.10).

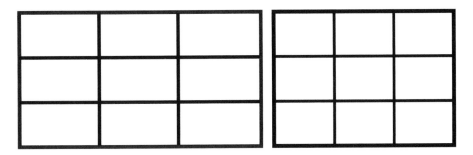

FIGURE 2.9   Frame markings along the 1/3 lines inside a 16:9 frame and a 4:3 frame.

The Rule of Thirds

FIGURE 2.10   Talent placed along the vertical 1/3 line.

Camera Angle

So now you should feel pretty comfortable composing simple subjects (human faces, etc.) within your frame. The rule of thirds, good headroom, and appropriate look room should already be giving you a well-balanced simple framing of the single human face based on our use of an objective shooting style. Although we have stopped our actor from looking directly into the lens and the head is turned at a slight angle, we are still photographing the talent from a frontal camera placement. This makes sense because you usually wish to place your camera at the most advantageous position to record the important details—in this case, the expression on the actor's face and the look in both of the eyes. There are times, however, when you need to move the camera around the actor and record the action from a different angle.

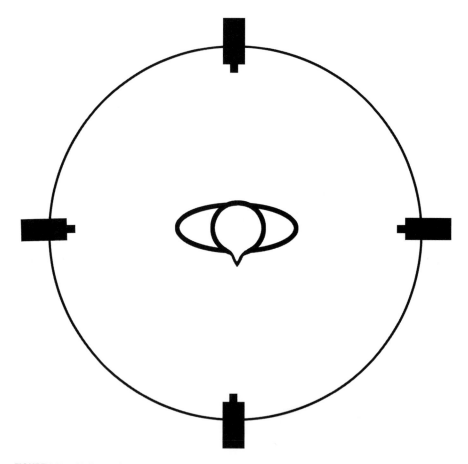

FIGURE 2.11 Bird's-eye view of camera's horizontal circle around talent.

We will explore the "**angles on action**" from two separate circles that surround your subject. The "angles on action" refer to the angle from which you photograph a person, event, or action. As we will see, the position of the camera and the view of our subject it offers the audience will impact how much information is conveyed and also the perceived meaning absorbed by the viewer. First, we will work our way around the actor along a horizontal circle, where the actor is the center and our camera traces the circumference (see Figure 2.11). Then we will explore a vertical circle, where the actor is the center and our camera will move above or below the horizon line to show our subject from a low or high angle (see Figure 2.12).

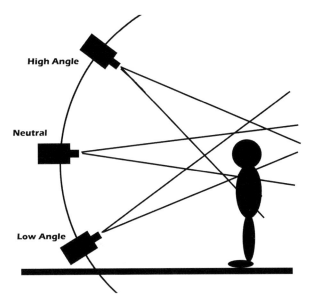

FIGURE 2.12   Side view of camera tracing path along vertical circle around talent. It is used to create high and low angle shots.

Camera Angle

Horizontal Camera Angles

As mentioned earlier, when you photograph a person directly from the front of their face, it often yields a rather flat, uninteresting image (depending on lighting, which we will touch upon later). An easy fix to this is to ask the talent to angle their face/eyes away from the camera lens. Keep in mind, however, that the camera, instead, can also be moved around the subject. Let us imagine that the talent is at the center of a circle, like the hub of a bicycle wheel laying flat. The camera, facing inward, can then move around that circle's center, at the circumference, or the end of the spokes where the rubber of the bicycle wheel would be. As there are 360 degrees in a circle, let us use the degrees to help define how far along the circumference we can move the camera and what kind of shot that would create (see Figure 2.13).

With the camera facing the talent at the zero degree mark, we would have a full frontal shot—flat and often uninteresting, but factual as in a news report. If the talent remains stationary and the camera begins to move around the subject along the arc of the circle to the talent's left side, then we go through the positive degrees (+45, +90, etc.) until the camera comes to the backside of the talent and sees only the back of the head at +180 degrees (Figure 2.14). The same type of arc can be made around the circle on the talent's right side and the degrees would progress the same but in negative values (−45, −90, −180) (Figure 2.15).

It might be easier to think of the degrees of the circle like the face of a clock where the actor is at the center of the hands and the camera is at the outer ring of numbers.

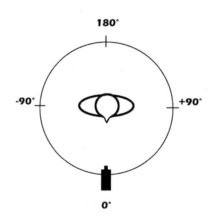

FIGURE 2.13 Camera's horizontal circle divided into degrees.

In this case, you could use the call outs of six o'clock for full frontal, three o'clock for left profile, nine o'clock for right profile, and twelve o'clock for full back of head (Figure 2.16).

Many people simply use a family of rough camera positions around talent, such as frontal, 3/4 front, left or right profile, 3/4 back, and from behind (Figure 2.17).

Remember from our earlier discussion that frontal shooting is used a great deal in non-fiction production as with news reporters and talk show hosts, but you will see it used often in fictional filmmaking when the talent walk toward camera or when they are driving a car with a **hood mount** and stare straight out past the camera as though they were actually driving. Although the audience gets to see the entire face, the overall image (depending on style of lighting used) can seem flat and lack a dynamic dimension, but shooting from the front is often necessary and appropriate—you just would not have the talent address the camera lens directly.

Horizontal Camera Angles

FIGURE 2.14 Camera's horizontal arc along positive angles.

FIGURE 2.15 Camera's horizontal arc along negative angles.

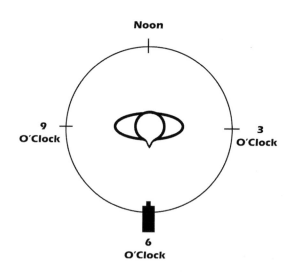

FIGURE 2.16 The numbers of the clock face can represent camera positions around the talent.

FIGURE 2.17   Frontal camera angle.

FIGURE 2.18   The 3/4 front left camera angle.

The 3/4 front, or 3/4 profile as some call it, is the most common angle on talent in fictional filmmaking. It provides the audience with a clear view of the front of talent so that facial expressions, hand gestures, and the like may be plainly seen. It also provides the frame with an increased degree of dimension. In closer shots of the human face, it brings out the contours and depth of the facial structures (eyes, nose, mouth, cheek bones, brow, jaw, ear, etc.). Note that we placed the camera around the circle to achieve the 3/4 frontal view of talent, but also placed the head and eyes along the line of thirds, yielding appropriate headroom and ample look room (Figure 2.18).

FIGURE 2.19 Talent in profile.

What kind of information can you get from the profile shot? You see if it is a man or a woman. You see the hair. If the person speaks, you will see the mouth open and close from the side. But unless your talent can migrate both eyes to one side of his head, like a flounder, the audience will not be privileged enough to see what the character might really be thinking or feeling. Since the eyes are the windows to the soul, not showing your audience the eyes (and full facial expressions) of an actor can generate feelings of duplicity, distrust, emotional disconnect, or secrecy. If this is the desired result you seek, then by all means use the profile shot, but otherwise, keep it reserved for these special occasions (Figure 2.19).

Now the 3/4 back shot should seem familiar to most of you. When used in tighter shots like we have here, it is getting to look more like what is called an **over-the-shoulder** shot (OTS). The camera gets to peek over the shoulder of our main talent and assumes a point of view like that of our talent (Figure 2.20). The camera (and therefore the viewing audience) sees directly what the main talent sees. Granted, the face of the actor is hidden from view, so we do not know what he or she may be thinking or feeling from this angle, but since the audience is placed into the shot from the character's **point-of-view** (POV), the audience is encouraged to do the thinking and feeling for the character or as the character more directly. This is sort of an objective–subjective shot type where you get a privileged point of view from what is usually a more neutral camera angle.

You may rarely have a need to frame a shot of an individual from fully behind them, but if you do, remember that the usual rules apply—headroom, look room, rule of thirds, etc.

FIGURE 2.20   The 3/4 back camera angle on talent.

FIGURE 2.21   Full back camera angle on talent.

As you may have already guessed, this type of shot totally obscures the talent's face and therefore keeps hidden the real thoughts, feelings, and intentions of this character. If, however, this is a known character placed in a suspenseful situation in the narrative, then this type of shot takes on a very subjective point of view, as though someone or something were following our hero from behind and is just about to strike. Scary stuff (Figure 2.21).

Horizontal Camera Angles

Vertical Camera Angles

In our examples thus far, the camera has been on an even plane with the object of interest—our actor's head. In other words, if his head is 4 feet off the ground then our camera and the **taking lens** (the lens that is actually recording the image) are also 4 feet off the ground (see Figure 2.22).

The general guideline to follow is that the camera and its lens should be looking at the subject from the same horizontal plane as the subject's eyes. This generates a neutral angle on action. The camera is positioned to observe the people, actions, or events from the same height as where the people exist or where the action takes place. An audience can better relate to the characters as equals. Once you raise the camera position above your actors or actions, or drop the camera below them, you begin to create a privileged point of view that results in a power dynamic within the shot. Let us explore both options (Figure 2.23).

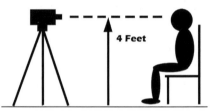

FIGURE 2.22   Camera height and angle of coverage traditionally fall at same height as talent's head for a neutral angle on action.

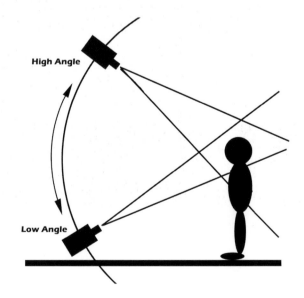

FIGURE 2.23   Vertical camera angles: high and low.

High Angle Shot

Covering any shot of a person or action from a higher vantage point immediately informs the audience of an implied meaning. The grammar of a high angle shot often yields an understanding within the viewer that who they are seeing on screen is smaller, weaker, subservient, diminutive, or is currently in a less powerful or compromised position. Through **foreshortening** and through "compressing" the character into the floor or ground around them, the camera keeps the subject down and makes him or her physically appear shorter or smaller (Figure 2.24).

If the high angle shot represents a point-of-view shot from another character, then the implied meaning is that the character that is up higher in the film's world is looking down on the other character both literally and figuratively. This POV may come from many entities such as a king, a giant, a flying creature, or an alien ship. An up/down power dynamic is created. Of course, there are few absolutes in film grammar and it is quite possible that when a character is seen from above, they may simply be occupying a physical location lower in the film space and therefore below the camera's placement. One will also find that a slightly higher camera angle down on talent yields a more pleasing line of the nose and jaw, and as a camera person you will often strive to make your talent look as good as possible.

FIGURE 2.24 A high angle view of talent.

High Angle Shot

Low Angle Shot

Let us now go in the opposite direction and drop the camera and lens below the neutral point and shoot from a lower angle up onto our person or action. As you may have already guessed, this angle on action usually generates the reverse feeling in your audience member. The character seen from below becomes larger, more looming, more significant, more powerful, and, of course, also physically higher in the film space. It is part of the accepted film grammar that a shot from below implies that the person or object you observe from that angle has a substantial presence, is considered larger than life, or may, at that point in the narrative, have the upper hand (literally and figuratively) (Figure 2.25).

The low angle as a POV shot also implies that the person (camera) doing that low angle observation is smaller, weaker, or in a more compromised position (think of someone who fell into a pit trap looking up at the person who set the trap for them—clearly a situation where the film space and narrative allows for the use of these shots—a low angle up to the higher person and then a reverse from the high shot down to the lower person). Again, it should be pointed out that sometimes a character is just at a higher elevation than other characters and it may not imply great importance, simply higher elevation.

It would be good to draw a distinction between a low angle shot and a shot that has a neutral angle but is taken from floor or ground level. The tilt of the actual camera lens determines what the shot becomes. If a baby sits on the floor and the camera is placed

FIGURE 2.25 A low angle view of talent.

on the floor at the same height as the baby and the lens on the camera is parallel to the floor, then you have a neutral angle on the subject—even though the legs of adults walking behind the baby may seem like those of large, looming giants (Figure 2.26). If the baby stays seated on the floor and the camera drops even lower and angles the lens up and away from the floor (any angle above the horizon line), then the camera has assumed a low angle position shooting up on to the large, looming giant adult legs, yielding that more diminutive sense of POV from the baby's position (Figure 2.27).

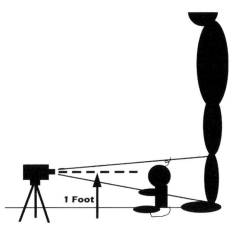

FIGURE 2.26   Camera lens parallel to ground is a neutral angle.

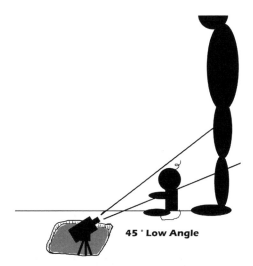

Low Angle Shot

FIGURE 2.27   Camera lens is tilted up away from floor and becomes a low angle shot.

The Two-Shot: Frame Composition with Two People

So far our basic shot types have been composed around one person. What happens when you need to include two people in a single frame? Well, as you have probably already guessed, you follow the same rules used for the single subject. Headroom, look room, rule of thirds, balance of weighted objects, and so forth all apply to a shot that must encompass two people having some interaction. The nature of the physical interaction, of course, also helps dictate what type of framing must be used and what type of **two-shot** will be composed.

The Profile Two-Shot

Perhaps the most common variety of two-shot, the profile two-shot, is used quite often to help set up a dialogue between two people in a scene. A long shot or medium long shot will most successfully cover all of the action during the meeting of the two characters. As the figures are smaller and the environment is more prominent, the setting can be established and larger body movements may be covered from these shot types. Common scenarios where the profile two-shot may be appropriate might be a meeting of two old friends on a street (Figure 2.28), a confrontation between two feuding characters, or a romantic dinner for two over a small, candle-lit table (Figure 2.29).

When using a tighter framing to compose a profile two-shot, you alter the implied meaning of the encounter by enclosing the characters in a much smaller space. A medium close-up or a close-up will force the faces of the characters together in an unnatural way, unless there is an obvious aggressive intention or an intimate overtone. Based on our previous examples, the confrontation (Figure 2.30) and the romantic dinner (Figure 2.31) may be good candidates for the medium close-up profile two-shot, but the meeting between the two old friends may not be well served by that framing. Forcing the faces of two characters together in a tight frame, when there is no real reason to do so, can make the viewing audience feel subconsciously uneasy.

FIGURE 2.28   Profile two-shot as composed for the long shot.

The Profile Two-Shot

FIGURE 2.29 Profile two-shot as composed for the medium long shot.

FIGURE 2.30 Medium close-up brings the feuding characters very close together in this profile two-shot.

FIGURE 2.31   Medium close-up serves to unite the romantic couple within the tighter frame.

The Direct to Camera Two-Shot

Whenever two people stand side by side and face the camera, you generate a more subjective shot. Their attention is toward the lens and not necessarily toward one another. An example of a truly subjective direct to camera two-shot would be two news anchors or sportscasters sitting side by side, addressing the viewing audience directly. A less subjective example would be two characters walking side by side down a city sidewalk approaching the camera (Figure 2.32) or perhaps two characters sitting in the front seats of a motor vehicle (Figure 2.33). These players have their bodies and faces

FIGURE 2.32   The medium long shot allows for ample room to move in this direct to camera two-shot.

FIGURE 2.33   A very common type of direct to camera two-shot. The confines of the car interior dictate the distance between the two characters facing the same camera.

opened up to the camera but, thanks to the conventions of fictional narrative objective shooting styles, they are not directly addressing the camera's lens or speaking directly to the viewing audience.

Either way, the framing for this type of shot must be wide enough to accommodate the shoulder width of the two people. The 16:9 wide screen aspect ratio of HD video will certainly help with this, but a medium shot may be the closest shot type that could be used to adequately frame for a direct to camera two-shot. Attempting to frame any tighter will necessitate the use of overlapping one body behind the other and establishing a visual "favor" for the character in the unobstructed frontal position. In this case, "favor" may establish a more dominant character in the story or it may just prove a convenient way of seeing a more intimate view of faces within one shot.

The Direct to Camera Two-Shot

The Over-the-Shoulder Two-Shot

Most often edited into a scene after the audience has first viewed the wider profile two-shot, the OTS two-shot favors one character's face by shooting from behind and slightly to the side of the other character's head. Because the profile two-shot establishes location and the two characters involved in the dialogue, the OTS shot allows for the audience to focus more attention on the one favored individual's face and script line delivery. In both previous versions of the two-shot, an audience member would have to choose between which character's face they would look at and when, but the OTS decides that for them.

An over-the-shoulder two-shot may be composed appropriately within a variety of shot types ranging from the long shot to the medium close-up. The most commonly used framing, however, is the MCU (Figures 2.34 and 2.35). It allows for good body composition, equal headroom and maintains the screen direction of look room from one character to the other. The wider aspect ratio of 16:9 may allow for a tighter framing of an OTS, but it runs the risk of compromising good composition in favor of more facial detail—a standard single close-up may be more appropriate, as the audience benefits little from seeing the possibly blurry slice of the back of the other character's head in the corner of the shot.

Often, as a filmmaker, you will have to ask your talent to stand unnaturally close to one another in order to achieve the two-shot framing you are seeking. This holds especially

FIGURE 2.34   Standard, medium close-up over-the-shoulder shot.

true for the over-the-shoulder shot. In real life it may look strange, but on the recorded image it will look appropriate to the viewing audience. Just be aware that in film language, proximity and grouping equate a unity between characters. The family of two-shots covers some pretty standard shots though and is often the best choice for recording different angles of the same conversation between two characters.

FIGURE 2.35   The tighter framing takes away from the efficacy of the over-the-shoulder shot.

Wrapping up the Basics of Composition

So the basics of frame composition are relatively simple. We have demonstrated them using several simple shot types covering one person placed "properly" within the frame. The two-shot brings into the frame a second subject but still follows the same rules. The basics of composition will apply to any of the wide variety of shot types and to any objects that you need to record. A vase with flowers should follow the same guidelines of composition—headroom, look room, rule of thirds, camera angle, etc. Once you know the shot types, the basics of framing, and the power behind camera angles, you are well on your way to using good film language and making well-balanced images for your motion pictures.

End of Chapter Two Review

1. Provide appropriate headroom for each shot type.
2. Decide if a subjective (to camera) or objective (not to camera) shooting style is more appropriate for your project.
3. Create ample look room for your subject to balance the weight of the frame.
4. Follow the rule of thirds and place important objects along the one-third lines within the frame, both horizontally and vertically.
5. Choose a horizontal camera angle around your subject for more meaningful coverage (the 3/4 profile being the most popular).
6. Shoot from a neutral, high, or low vertical camera angle to inform an audience about a character's "power dynamic."
7. Profile and direct to camera two-shots work best from long to medium shots, but over-the-shoulder two-shots will work best from the medium close-up.

Chapter Three
Composition—Beyond the Basics

QUESTION: How can a two-dimensional (2D) recorded image give the impression of three-dimensional (3D) space?

ANSWER: There are many ways to use compositional elements to create the illusion of three-dimensional space within the film or video frame. Many popular methods include diagonal lines, foreground and background objects, object size, atmospherics, wide or long lenses, focus, and lighting.

Up until now we have kept most of our compositions very basic—a single person standing in a simple environment. Clearly you will be creating much more elaborate shots for your own projects, but we all have to start with the basic rules of visual grammar. By this point you should feel comfortable with your camera's aspect ratio, the multiplicity of shot types, the rule of thirds, headroom, look room, and camera angles on action. This chapter builds on this grammar and introduces new and more compelling ways to fill your shot compositions with information, meaning, and beauty.

The Third Dimension

As we have said, the film or video camera captures a flat, two-dimensional image and the movie theatre, television, and computer screens display a flat, two-dimensional image. So how is it that when we watch television and, more noticeably, movies on very large theatre screens that the elements of the frame (either static or moving) seem to occupy a three-dimensional space? Well, the simple answer is to say that this phenomenon is achieved through visual illusions and tricks for the human eye and brain. There are many more in-depth physiological and psychological reasons, but this is not the appropriate place to explore those topics fully. Feel free to do your own research on the human visual system and how we interpret light, color, motion, depth, and so forth.

What we can discuss briefly is how our human visual system differs from the visual system of a film or video camera. On the most simplistic level it comes down to how many lenses get used to create the image. Humans have two eyes on the front of their heads, and the eyes are spaced several inches apart from one another. This configuration results in binocular vision (bi meaning "two" and ocular referring to the "eye"). Binocular vision allows us to establish depth in our visual space by causing us to see the same objects from two separate vantage points. Each eye sees the same objects from slightly different horizontal positions and therefore "captures" a slightly different

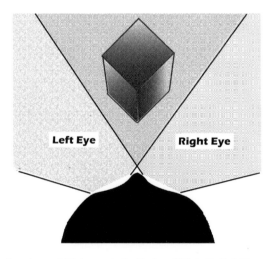

FIGURE 3.1 Each eye's vantage point helps create the illusion of 3D depth. Test this yourself by holding any 3D object about 1.5 feet in front of your face, making sure that it is askew and not perfectly flat to your vision, then alternately open one eye and look at the object and then close that eye and open the other eye to see the same object—note how the two views of this close object are different.

picture—offset by those several inches of distance between the two eyes in the head. The brain then unites those two separate pictures and generates one view of the world around us rendered with the three-dimensional perspective (Figure 3.1).

Most film and video cameras, of course, only have one eye—the single taking lens—so they are unable to record the same type of three-dimensional space as the human eye. Therefore, filmmakers must generate the illusion of multidimensionality. The illusion of depth on the 2D plane of film or video can be created in many ways. For now, let us explore how to be great 3D illusionists with our shots.

The Third Dimension

The Horizon Line

We are going to leave our human subjects aside for the time being and put our attention into shooting a generic exterior. Shot-wise we are talking about the long shot family, especially the extreme long shot (XLS). Depending on the surrounding topography of your shoot location and your camera angle, this shot should result in capturing a large field of view of the world—the ground, the sky, and many things within those zones. For illustrative purposes we will keep the environment rather bare and start with just a **horizon line** (Figure 3.2).

The horizon line is what keeps a viewer locked in a knowable spatial relationship with the film space. In other words, it keeps them grounded by allowing for a clear up/down and left/right orientation. Your major goal should be to keep your horizon line as level as possible and in alignment with—parallel to—the top and bottom edges of your physical film or video frame. This is relatively easy to do by eye when you are shooting an Earth-bound project, but what happens when you begin to shoot in outer space? Where is the horizon established then? That is something for you to ponder on your own. For now, we will stick to the surface of the Earth and keep things level. You will see that the aforementioned illustration (Figure 3.2) accomplishes this goal, but let us add actual objects to help further discuss horizon line and composition (Figure 3.3).

Now we can begin to appreciate what the level horizon line is doing for our picture composition. Figure 3.3 shows a frame cut directly in half along the vertical—the horizon

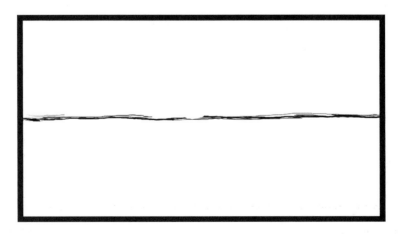

FIGURE 3.2   A simple horizon line bisecting the vertical plane of the frame.

bisects the frame separating top from bottom. There is headroom for the mountains, sun, and clouds, but does the image follow the rule of thirds? Does it have to? Horizon lines may be placed across your frame wherever you see fit, but its placement will allow you to highlight more sky and less ground or less sky and more ground. If we tilt the camera angle down, we push the horizon line up in our frame (Figure 3.4). If we tilt the camera angle up, we push the horizon line down in our frame (Figure 3.5). Each of these examples shows the horizon line following the rule of thirds. To many, this is a more pleasing position within the frame.

FIGURE 3.3   Adding visible objects to your horizon line frame helps establish place, time, and physical scale.

The Horizon Line

FIGURE 3.4   By tilting the vertical camera angle down, the horizon line now falls along the upper one-third of the frame, resulting in less headroom for the mountains and sky.

FIGURE 3.5 By tilting the vertical camera angle up, the horizon line now falls along the lower one-third of the frame, resulting in more visible space for the mountains and sky.

Dutch Angle

You will most often strive to keep your horizon line stable and level, thus ensuring an even viewing plane for your audience. A shift in your horizon line is also likely to cause shifts in your vertical lines—any tall building, tree, door frame, and so on will look tilted or slanted, not upright and even. When horizontal and vertical lines go askew it causes a sense of uneasiness and a slight disorientation in your audience. If this is done unintentionally, then you get people confused. Done on purpose and you have created what is called a **Dutch angle**, a **Dutch tilt**, a **canted angle**, or an **oblique angle**. When a character is sick or drugged or when a situation is "not quite right" you may choose to tilt the camera left or right and create this nonlevel horizon. The imbalance will make the viewer feel how unstable the character or environment really is—visuals underscore the story (Figure 3.6).

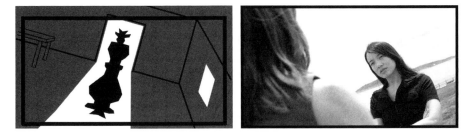

FIGURE 3.6 Examples of Dutch angle or canted angle shots. Note how the slanted horizontal and vertical lines skew the balance of the image. Something is not quite right within the story at this point.

Diagonal Lines

So far, all of these horizon line examples have been locked in two-dimensional frames. The strong horizontal line, one-third down the screen from the top, is a good compositional start, but it does not create depth. You need to establish that this XLS captures depth in the physical world of the filmed image. To help with this goal, you could employ an old artist's trick called the **vanishing point**. In our current example, we could have placed our camera in the center of a two-lane highway that stretches straight out to the horizon. For the most part, roads have a consistent width and therefore the lines that represent the edges of the roadway should be parallel to one another for as long as the road covers the ground. When observed across a large distance, however, the edge lines seem to get closer and closer together until they appear to merge at the horizon. This place along the horizon where parallel lines appear to merge together is the vanishing point (see Figure 3.7).

This simple illustration represents the receding roadway with two diagonal lines. Again, in reality, the road's width should be constant, but as we observe in reality, in drawings, and on a filmed image, when viewed over a long distance, the lines of the road appear to converge. This is, of course, an illusion. The key thing to realize here is that the diagonal lines bring that illusion of depth to our frame. So, whenever you can employ diagonal lines within your composition (a road, a hallway, a line of people

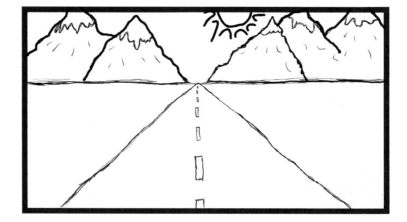

FIGURE 3.7   The straight road vanishes at the horizon line, implying that a great distance is visible and the space within the frame now yields the illusion of the third dimension of depth.

waiting for the bus) you are creating the impression of three-dimensional space on the two-dimensional film frame.

This does not mean that you must always use diagonal lines, however. Yes, they are compositionally bold elements within your frame and yes they can create depth, but what if your goal is to create a shot that has no depth? You want your character to appear in a flat space, like up against a wall—reflecting the story's subtext and psychological meaning—she is trapped or she is not capable of moving in a dynamic direction at this point of the narrative (Figure 3.8).

To achieve the shot in Figure 3.8, the camera had to be placed at the height of the actor and perpendicular to the wall itself. This frame, flat on to a wall, has no real sense of depth. The full frontal angle on action only shows some horizontal lines on the wall. The person is enclosed by the environment and can only move left or right, or potentially toward camera. In this instance, the absence of perceived depth adds to the mental or emotional state of the character. The composition of the shot underscores the state of being for the character recorded within it.

A slight shift in the camera's angle on action (horizontal repositioning) yields a different image with a different meaning. It shows the same woman in front of the same wall, but now a diagonal line exists, as does a distant horizon. With the frame opened up this way, the character has more options for movement—left, right, near, or far.

Diagonal Lines

FIGURE 3.8 The person, framed up against a flat wall, seems boxed in or trapped by the environment. Although visually uninteresting to many, this shot can convey hidden meaning about the character in the story.

Depth is created because we can now see out into the world along those diagonal lines that draw the viewer's eye away from the main character and out into the deep space of the film world—an illusion of the third dimension is created on the flat film frame (Figure 3.9).

FIGURE 3.9 By shooting the same woman by the same wall from a different camera angle, we now unlock the diagonal lines, which lead the eye into the depth of the "3D" shot. The meaning of the shot and the character's mental state may now be different.

The Depth of Film Space—Foreground/Middle Ground/Background

The diagonal lines framed within a shot help draw a viewer's eye from objects close to the camera to objects further away from the camera, or deeper into the film's space. This space is divided into three sections based on the proximity to the camera's taking lens: **foreground** (FG), **middle ground** (MG), and **background** (BG). Together with the borders of the frame they help form the film's three-dimensional space: height, width, and depth.

Foreground

As the name implies, the FG is the zone between the camera's lens and the main subject being photographed. It is the space before the area of interest. Nothing has to occupy this space and often it is simply filled with empty air. A creative film person, however, can choose to place something in that space. Of course, a foreground element must enhance the composition of the shot and should not obscure the zones behind it. The object may serve to help set the environment (a tree branch), it may be an abstract shape (part of a wall or a park bench), and it may also carry meaning for the narrative (a stop sign at a crossroads). Whatever the object and whatever the purpose, you should try very hard to not have arbitrary or accidental foreground elements because they may distract your viewer from observing the more important details that are staged deeper in your shot (Figure 3.10).

FIGURE 3.10 The stop sign occupies a noticeable area of the shot's foreground zone. It appears large because it is closer to the camera. Because it obscures objects behind it, it helps provide a sense of depth within the frame.

Middle Ground

Regardless of the size of your shooting location, the majority of your important action will occupy the middle ground. This is the zone where dialogue can unfold, a couple can dance, or a car can pull up to a stop sign. All or most of the physical action is visible within the frame. An audience member is likely to receive all of the information within the shot when the main action is staged here. Middle ground is much easier to establish in wider shots such as medium and long shots. The close-up family of shot types gets trickier to find the depth to show all three ground zones, but it is still possible if you plan well (Figure 3.11).

Background

Since you now understand foreground and middle ground, it will be easy to guess what the background is—everything behind the MG out to infinity. Of course, if you are shooting inside a restaurant then there will be no "infinity" but the physical space behind the main action being recorded will be the background. The other patrons eating, the servers walking about, and the wall at the back end of the room all become part of the shot's background. This zone can be rather barren, like the dunes of a desert, or rather busy, like the commotion found along a city's avenue. When shooting on location, you may be limited by how much you can control the BG, but you should try hard to frame your shots so that the background does not overpower the main action in the middle ground. In our previous illustrative examples, the simple mountain range in the distance has served as the shot's background all along.

FIGURE 3.11 The car now occupies an area of interest inside the middle ground of this shot.

Depth Cues

The combination of foreground, middle ground, and background elements helps create the illusion of three dimensions on the 2D film frame. They accomplish this in a few ways. First, they act like layers. The tree branch in the foreground will partially obscure the elements of the MG and BG. The main action taking place in the MG will obscure visual elements found in the BG zone. So, just like in real life, when objects (static or moving) appear to be in front of one another it allows our brains to establish depth cues. Second, the relative size of a known object will also trigger depth cues. For instance, you may observe a small skyscraper within the shot. Because skyscrapers are known to be very tall buildings, it would make sense to assume that this structure actually lived in the background zone relatively far away from the camera. However, if you placed a miniature toy model of a skyscraper in the foreground, you would achieve a similar BG assumption but it would be the result of an optical illusion where scale and perspective were tricking the eye and the brain's sense of depth.

Another depth cue, found especially in exterior wide or long shots, is **atmosphere (or atmospherics)**. If you have ever looked up a long street in the city or stood atop a hill in the country and stared off toward the horizon, then you may have experienced the dissatisfaction of a less than clear view. Perhaps the distant hills or distant buildings seemed cloudy or even totally obscured. This is often the result of what are called atmospherics—the presence of particulates suspended in the air. This is most often water vapor, but it may be smoke from a nearby fire, dust, pollen, or even pollutants. When you stand in this atmosphere, it may not obscure your vision of local objects very much, but when viewed across a greater expanse (as in an XLS) the cumulative effect of the particles in the air causes distant objects to be obscured. If you were to record a shot in such an environment, the viewing audience would immediately understand the depth cue. Fog machines are often employed for just such a purpose on film sets.

Depth Cues

The Camera Lens—The Eye in Composition

Let us switch gears a bit and put some attention toward an extremely important piece of visual storytelling equipment—the camera lens. There would be no grammar of the shots if there were no lens on the camera to record those shots. In the most simplistic terms, the job of the camera lens is to collect light rays bouncing off the world in front of the camera (the scene you are shooting) and focus those light rays on to whatever recording medium you are using (emulsion film or a video camera's electronic sensor). It can be that simple, yet the job of the lens, the type of lenses, and the quality of lenses can vary widely.

Remember that it is through your lens that your composition is created, and depending on how you use your lens, you can achieve different looks or results with the composition and the film space. Because we do not have the time to delve deeply into the history and current technology of film and video camera lenses, we will try to touch on the main points of interest that will help you make good decisions about your shots and about what the lens choice does for the grammar of those shots.

The Zoom Lens

Most likely you will be shooting your projects with some format of video camera (such as mini-DV or HDV perhaps) and that camera will most likely have a built-in lens and that lens will most likely be a zoom lens. The zoom lens is very popular, especially with video cameras, because the one lens allows you to create a variety of shot frames— from a wide shot with a wide field of view of the world to a tighter, more magnified narrow field of view. On your camera's zoom control, the wide end of the lens view is usually marked with a "W" (for wide) and the narrow or magnified end of the lens view is usually marked "T" (for telephoto). When the camera stays locked in place physically and you use the zoom to change your framing view from wide to telephoto, you are actually magnifying some small section of the original wide field of view and the result is an enlarged detail within the tighter shot.

The zoom lens is a complicated construction of many glass elements and telescoping barrels or rings that all work together to collect light from the wide field of view, from the opposite end's most narrow field of view, and from all the fields of view in between. The term **focal length** is used most often to discuss how wide or how telephoto a zoom lens might frame the shot, and the measurement for focal length is usually done in millimeters (mm). So if you see a lower number in millimeters (such as 10 or 16mm) associated with a zoom lens, then that lower number is referencing the wide end of the zoom range. Therefore, a higher number (such as 75 or 150mm) represents the narrow or highly magnified end of the zoom range.

Until this point, without really having drawn attention to it, our discussions of shot types, framing, and composition have all been based on camera proximity to subject. This means that if we had wanted to frame a CU shot we would have either moved the camera closer to the talent or moved the talent closer to the camera. This is just like your own eyes. If you want to see something in more detail you must move closer to it or move it closer to your eyes. The obvious point here is that we do not have zoom capabilities with our human eyes. We have one focal length to our vision, which is often referred to as "**normal**." We manufacture camera lenses to also have this "normal" field of view (in between the extremes of the wide end and narrow end of the zoom range), and it has been with this view that we have framed up all of our shots so far. They appear natural or neutral in their perspective on the subject or scene shown, just as if they had been recorded through a pair of human eyes. Without getting too technical, the "normal" camera lens angle of view depends on the focal length of the lens, the diameter of lens, and the size of the format (16mm, 35mm film/SD or HD video).

All this discussion leads up to one key point, and that is the feeling your shot conveys to an audience is also dependent upon what focal length is used to record the image and how close the camera is to the subject being recorded with that focal length. The normal or neutral field of view captures the shot as if we were there personally, observing the action rather than the camera. As soon as you move to the extremes of the zoom range, however, the science behind lens optics and optical illusions starts to creep in.

A wide angle shot from the short end of the focal length range alters the perspective on the scene being shot. It exaggerates space and appears to expand the depth of the shot, therefore playing up the 3D perspective of the image. A telephoto angle shot from the long end of the focal length range deemphasizes 3D space and compresses visual elements from the foreground–middle ground–background into a much tighter "space" lacking some of the 3D perspective (see Figures 3.12, 3.13, and 3.14). Much like in still portraiture photography, it may be advisable to shoot your talent's close-up shots with a slightly longer focal length lens from further away so that you do not exaggerate their features (enlarged nose, receding ears, etc.).

The Zoom Lens

Of course, the more extreme the focal length, the more distorted the image's perspective will appear. This holds especially true for short focal length, very wide angle lenses (sometimes called "fisheye" lenses) where they can really warp the depth cues of your shot and exaggerate the 3D space. The grammar of shots like these tells your viewer that there is a warped or distorted view of the film world going on. Something is not quite right. Perhaps it is a nightmare sequence or a fantasy episode or a character is thinking or behaving in an altered state of some kind. Whatever the creative visual reason, it certainly is not "normal."

Results like those shown in Figure 3.15 are also enhanced by camera placement and focal length choice. When you combine a wide lens with a camera in close to the

FIGURE 3.12   A long focal length shot. Note the compression of space.

FIGURE 3.13   A midrange zoom "normal" focal length shot.

subject, you get this very exaggerated perspective. When you combine a long lens with subjects further away from the camera, you get a more compressed perspective (see Figure 3.12). This compression can imply a "tight" or "flat" life being led by a character or a place that is constraining or prison-like, especially since the "slice" of background or environment around your subject is also small and confining. Either way, your audience can glean additional meaning from your shot depending on what end of the zoom range you use.

FIGURE 3.14   A wide angle focal length shot. Note the increased depth perspective.

FIGURE 3.15   "Fisheye" lens distortion. An ultrawide angle lens very close to your subject can yield this sort of physical distortion within your image. A surreal, comical, or fantastical feeling may be generated by this lens choice.

The Zoom Lens

Lens Focus—Directing the Viewer's Eye Around Your Frame

We now understand that the framing of a shot is established through camera format, camera angle, camera proximity, and camera lens focal length. The composition of objects and/or subjects within that frame is your creative goal, and you are now staging those elements along the rule of thirds and diagonal lines deep into the frame's middle ground and background. Utilizing this deep space in your film frame also allows you to unlock an additional tool in your shot construction tool kit—**focus**.

Your eyes can only focus on one thing at a time. As you look from one place around you to another, your eye instantly changes focus to the new distance of the new object of visual interest. The illusion of constant focus is achieved, but, in reality, you are only able to focus on one physical plane or distance from your eye at any one time. A camera lens behaves in the same way. It can only generate clear, crisp focus at one distance from the camera at one time. This distance is called the **point of critical focus**. There is a zone around this distance of critical focus that may also appear to be in acceptable focus (not yet blurry), and this zone is called the **depth of field** (DOF). Lucky for you, image optics follow certain scientific rules, so there are many charts and tables available to help you predict this changing depth of field and they allow you to creatively set what may be in focus within your frame.

Setting focus is the job of the camera operator or camera assistant. Determining what important object within the composition of the frame gets treated to the primary critical focus is often the job of the director or the director of photography. As staging talent and set dressing deep into the shot are now possible, you get to determine where (what distance from the camera) the focus is set and therefore control what the viewing audience will most likely pay attention to on the screen. Another bit of shot grammar for you here: what is in focus in your shot is the important thing for the viewer to watch.

Again, humans pretty much see everything in focus all of the time. We are not accustomed to seeing things blurry (unless we need corrective lenses and choose not to wear them). A camera lens does not know what is or what should be in focus. Only you, the camera operator, knows that. You set the critical plane of focus and the corresponding depth of field according to what you wish to have in proper focus. The audience will want to look at the objects within that zone of most clear and crisp focus. Anything outside the depth of field will appear blurry to the viewer's eye and therefore not be an attractive element to watch.

As you can see, selecting the focus object is a key component to directing your viewer's experience as they watch the elements within your frame. Because the human face and eyes are usually the main objects of interest, you may wish to keep the DOF narrow and blur out the possibly distracting BG. This way, the audience pays attention to the actor and not the sign on the wall thirty feet behind him. But be careful when setting focus, because soft focus or slightly blurry shots are easily noticed by the keen eyes of the viewer, and unless there is an immediate correction or introduction of some element within the frame that comes into clear focus, the viewer will reject the shot and disassociate from the viewing experience. You have not done a very good job as a camera operator or director in that instance.

Pulling Focus vs Following Focus

Let us stay on the focus topic for just a bit longer so that you can pick up another technique to help you direct the viewer's attention within your shot. As a single shot plays itself out, and there are multiple subjects at differing distances from the camera, it is possible to shift the focus from one subject to the other as the action unfolds and is recorded. This practice is called **pulling focus** or **pushing focus,** depending on what direction you have to move the lens's focus ring in order to actually (optically) shift the focus from one distance to another in the depth of your shot. This practice is also often called **racking focus**. If your goal is to keep focus on one moving object within the frame of your shot, then you may call it **following focus**.

The fact that you have the option to pull focus or to follow focus means that not everything in your shot's FG, MG, and BG will be in focus at the same time. This scenario, complete acceptable focus through all three zones, is possible, but all these options are the result of your manipulation of the depth of field. The depth of field was mentioned earlier in this chapter, but let us examine it a bit more closely here. As we have learned, because the lens can only see one critical focus point, you can only create one plane (or slice of physical space in front of the lens at some distance) of exact, perfect focus. The DOF is a zone around that point of critical focus that will appear to be in acceptable focus.

The depth of field zone can grow larger to infinity or shrink smaller to just a few inches or centimeters. As a general rule of thumb, the DOF will be found roughly one-third in front of and two-thirds behind the plane of critical focus (see Figure 3.16).

What determines your DOF is a combination of various factors involved in capturing the image. In order to keep it simple, we will just say that the focal length of your lens, the

Lens Focus—Directing the Viewer's Eye Around Your Frame

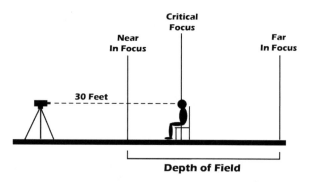

FIGURE 3.16   Critical focus set to main subject while depth of field occupies some distance roughly one-third in front of and two-thirds behind that critical focus plane.

Table 3.1–Factors that control the depth of field without regard to size of format

	Large Depth of Field	Small Depth of Field
Focal Length	Short (Wide)	Long (Narrow)
Camera to Subject Distance	Far	Near
Lens Aperture	Small (High Number)	Large (Low Number)

aperture (iris) set on the lens, the size of format (16mm/35mm film or SD/HD video), and the distance from the lens to the object of primary or critical focus all work together to determine the overall DOF. Let us explore the two extremes found in Table 3.1.

The logic follows that when you shoot a short focal length (wide angle) daylight exterior long shot, you will generate the largest possible DOF on your given lens. Most likely a few feet from the camera to infinity will be in acceptable focus. Conversely, when you shoot a long focal length (telephoto) nighttime interior XCU, you will generate the most shallow DOF. Perhaps only a few inches to a few centimeters might be seen in acceptable focus. You can employ tools such as **neutral density filters (ND filters)** on the lens to help lessen the amount of light entering the lens on daylight exteriors or you can add more light to your nighttime interiors in order to better control your DOF from shot to shot for more creative focus purposes (Figures 3.17 and 3.18).

FIGURE 3.17 A large depth of field allows all visual elements in the FG, MG, and BG to appear in rather sharp focus. This can often make it difficult for your viewer to know where to look for the most important visual information.

FIGURE 3.18 A shallow depth of field keeps the critical focus on the main subject and blurs the other elements outside the near and far distances of acceptable focus.

Lens Focus—Directing the Viewer's Eye Around Your Frame

Light in Composition—Now You See It, Now You Don't

In the last section we mentioned how creatively placing the area of crisp focus in the frame can lead the viewer's eye around your shot. This section briefly explores how light can be used to do the same thing. Values of light and dark can generate a sense of depth in the 2D frame; create feelings of sadness, happiness, fear and so on; underscore themes about characters; and highlight or obscure the more important subjects in a scene. All of this and more fall within the capabilities of film lighting. It will often be your most powerful creative tool in your filmmaking toolbox, but that does not mean it has to be the most complex or the most expensive. Learning about and using light effectively is a lifelong process so let us move ahead and address some of the basics to help get us started on our way.

In the natural world, humans are programmed to respond to light, movement, and color. It stands to reason then that while viewing a motion picture we would respond to these same three visual attributes, plus sharp focus. Knowing this physiological visual response of humans is a great creative tool for filmmakers to use in constructing good shot composition. It is very important for you to realize from the outset that well-planned and well-executed lighting can make or break the visual success of a motion picture project. When you approach your lighting design for a program, you should be thinking about an overall look, how the lighting can underscore or work against thematic tones, if the story requires a particular color palette or quality of light, and also what techniques might achieve these lighting requirements. Your final visual product will reflect these strong choices and your resultant lighting scheme will affect your viewing audience on yet another positive level.

The art and craft of film and video lighting is a huge topic that is well covered by many other qualified training manuals and film production text books. We do not have the luxury of addressing all of the scientific, technical, and aesthetic factoids about light and film lighting here, but we will hit on some of the more important terms and practices involved with the discipline regarding the grammar of the shot. The following list should set most of us on the right foot.

- Light as energy
- Color temperature
- Natural or artificial light
- Quantity of light: sensitivity and exposure
- Quality of light: soft vs hard
- Contrast
- Basic character lighting: three point method
- Set and location lighting

Light in Composition—Now You See It, Now You Don't

Light as Energy

Light, no matter what generates it, is energy—energy waves of electromagnetic radiation that happen to live in a zone of frequencies known as the **visible spectrum**. Light itself is invisible, but objects that reflect light can appear white, black, or combinations of colors or hues from violet, blue, green, yellow, orange, and red. When white light (all color wavelengths) hits an object and reflects all wavelengths equally, you see that object as white. If an object absorbs all light then the object is seen as black. When an object absorbs all colors but reflects yellow you see it as yellow. Not all light sources emit pure white light in a balanced spectrum but luckily we have ways of measuring the color of light.

Color Temperature

Color temperature, along the scale of **degrees Kelvin**, helps us understand what color the invisible light is. It is measured in the thousands of degrees (roughly 1000 to 20,000 degrees Kelvin). Without going into all the science behind it, you should just understand that there are two main colors of concern along the Kelvin scale for film and video shooting: reddish amber and blue. The numbers associated most commonly with their color temperatures are 3200 and 5600 degrees Kelvin, respectively. Film lights generally emit 3200 degrees Kelvin light, and noontime daylight (from the sun) is roughly around 5600 degrees Kelvin. The lower the number of degrees Kelvin (0–4000-ish), the more reddish, or "warmer," the light will be. The higher the number of degrees Kelvin (4000–10,000 and above), the bluer, or "cooler," the light will appear (Figure 3.19).

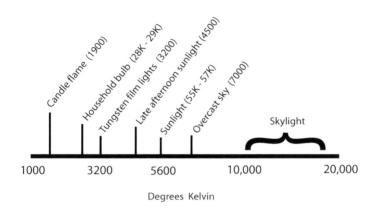

FIGURE 3.19   The Kelvin scale showing various examples of common color temperatures.

Natural or Artificial Light

These values of degrees Kelvin are extremely important to film shooting because the physical film emulsion is balanced by the manufacturer to want to see either 3200 degree light as "white" or 5600 degree light as "white." The balance toward 3200 is referred to as **tungsten balanced**, and the film that seeks 5600 degree light as white light is called **daylight balanced**. The electronic light sensors on most video cameras [**charge-coupled devices** (CCDs)] are also calibrated to record tungsten (3200) or daylight (5600) and often have a setting for both so you can switch back and forth as needed.

Now tungsten is called tungsten because it is the chief element in the metallic filament inside the light bulb (or lamp) that glows "white" hot when electricity is run through it. Many people also refer to this kind of light as film or quartz lighting and it is used chiefly in film and video making specifically. To clarify, however, any kind of light source generated by a man-made device can be called an **artificial light** even though it is not emitting 3200 degree Kelvin waves. Examples could include neon lights, a household incandescent or CFL, overhead fluorescent lighting, a computer or TV screen, street lights, car headlamps, a flashlight or hand torch, and so on. Because artificial lights produce a wide range of color temperature light, try to use the special film lights for your shooting or use all the same kind of lamp in multiple fixtures so you at least have consistent color output on your scene.

The bluer daylight calibration derives its name from its chief supplier, daylight, and is also called **natural light**. Natural light sources include the sun, moon, fire, candles (even though man-made), and so on. However, there are man-made film lighting fixtures (**HMI**s) that also emit light waves around the 5600–6000 degree Kelvin ballpark. These lights can be used to augment or replace natural sunlight/daylight. When shooting outdoors, an easy way to augment your light levels is to bounce or reflect the free and available light by using **bounce boards**, **bounce cards**, **shiny reflectors**, or **mirrors**.

You must be careful, however, which light sources you use with which color temperature-balanced film or video. If you give tungsten-balanced media (film or video) daylight energy waves, it will record with a bluish tint. If you give a daylight-balanced medium tungsten light, it will record as reddish. Generally, you should match the color temperature of your light source with the color temperature sensitivity of your film or video medium. It is also possible to mix natural and artificial lighting for creative or dramatic purposes. There are also a wide range of colored gelatin sheets that you can place on the lighting fixtures to alter or correct the color output of the raw lamp (Figure 3.20).

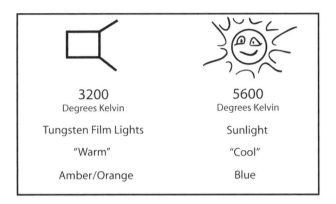

3200
Degrees Kelvin

Tungsten Film Lights

"Warm"

Amber/Orange

5600
Degrees Kelvin

Sunlight

"Cool"

Blue

FIGURE 3.20   The two main color temperatures for video and film.

Natural or Artificial Light

Quantity of Light: Sensitivity and Exposure

Light is needed for all motion picture production (emulsion film or video) because its presence, in the correct quantities, allows for correct exposure. This means that when a high enough quantity of light illuminates something in front of your lens, it can be seen and registered by the recording medium. You have to have enough light falling on your scene for it to be visible to your film or video CCD. The human visual system has a wide range of "exposure" sensitivity when it comes to lesser or greater amounts of light. We do not have to swap out our eyes for low light viewing nor do we consciously switch over our eyes for seeing in very bright light.

Film emulsions and video light sensors are not as widely flexible and are pretty much built to one sensitivity initially. We say initially because there are technical things that can be done to alter film and video sensitivity, but for our purposes we will assume the single sensitivity rating given by the manufacturer (often represented by a number calculated by the International Organization for Standardization or in the form of an exposure index or ASA rating). If you accidentally provide too much light to your camera you can **overexpose** the image and make it too bright or "blown out." If you do not provide enough light, you will **underexpose** and the image will be too dark (Figure 3.21).

Depending on the sensitivity rating of the film emulsions and video cameras you use, you may require more or less light on a subject to record it properly. A lower exposure rating number (50, 64, 100) means a less sensitive medium, whereas a higher number (320, 500) means a more sensitive medium. **Light meters** (either handheld devices or built into the video camera), which are calibrated to your medium's light sensitivity, are used to help measure the quantity of light falling on your subjects and film set. Opening or closing the lens iris (or aperture) is the most common way of controlling how much or how little light gets into the camera.

FIGURE 3.21 The range of exposures on one shot. "Proper" exposure is whatever the story calls for. Creatively speaking, you may wish to severely under- or overexpose a few shots for your film, but most should be in a moderate range exposure.

Achieving basic exposure of the elements within your shot is just the beginning. Achieving creative control over where, how much light, and what quality of light you place around your frame is your real goal. Light impacts many other creative choices. One easy lesson to remember about the quantity of light is that the more you have available on set, the larger your depth of field can be (think daytime exterior). You would have to "close down" your camera's iris to block out more of the available bright light, which, in turn, increases your DOF. The less light you have, the more shallow your depth of field will be when you "open up" your iris. So purposefully limiting the light used for proper exposure can alter what is in or out of focus in your shot, in addition to what is well exposed or not (Figure 3.22).

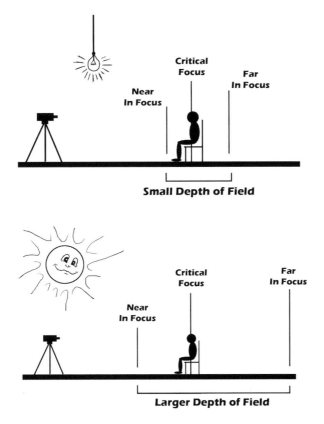

FIGURE 3.22 The amount of light on your scene directly impacts the depth of field focus range.

Quantity of Light: Sensitivity and Exposure

Quality of Light: Hard vs Soft

Beyond the color temperature and the quantity of light, most filmmakers are also concerned with the quality of the light. Not how good or how bad the light looks, although that is extremely important, but how hard or how soft the beams are that illuminate the actors and the set. If you have ever stood outside on a cloudless day you no doubt noticed how distinct your shadow was. A hard-edged shadow is the primary giveaway that you are using a **hard light** source. The sun, as a single **point source** light, sends its light waves to Earth and, for the most part, they are parallel to one another. They create a single, deep shadow with well-defined edges.

These parallel light waves are very directional and will illuminate one surface brightly, get blocked by that surface, and then not hit anything behind it, thus causing the hard-edged shadow. This does not mean that hard lights (with parallel rays) are brighter than softer lights, they are just more focused. The biggest and most readily available hard light source is our sun (on a cloudless day), and it is free for us to use so take advantage of it during your shooting as much as possible. Hard light, depending on its application, is often less pleasing on the human face and can cause harsh eye socket shadows (top light), highlight skin imperfections, and so on. Hard light can create scary, dangerous, harsh, or mysterious environments when used in motion pictures.

Soft light, however, is very diffused light. If you were to go outside on a cloudy, overcast day (with no direct sunlight visible) you would not easily see your shadow at all or, if you did, it would be very faint or not hard-edged. The hard, parallel rays of sunlight hit the clouds in the atmosphere and then get all jumbled up and diverted into many different directions and bounce around our atmosphere. This diffused light of multidirectional energy waves comes at objects from many sides and therefore it illuminates more evenly all around—not hard and directional from one side but soft and diffused

FIGURE 3.23 Examples of hard light and soft light.

from several sides. Almost any light source can become a soft light by diffusing it or bouncing it off walls or ceilings. Soft light sources tend to be more flattering to the human face because they cause little in the way of deep shadows with the light wrapping around the curves and shapes of the surfaces. Soft light also implies a sense of warmth, friendliness, or romance when used in motion pictures (Figure 3.23).

Quality of Light: Hard vs Soft

Contrast

If you stare at an all white wall, no visual contrast exists—everything is the same, a wash of white. If you then paint half that wall black you will create a very well-defined high contrast visual statement—white instantly turns into black along the painted edge between the two tones, resulting in half-bright values and half-dark values. Film lighting deals in similar terms, where **contrast** can mean the relative differences between light and dark areas within the frame. A high contrast image is an image that contains areas that are both very bright and very dark, with well-defined edges between the two. Conversely, a low contrast image contains more even lighting levels across the whole frame such that the delineation between light and dark regions is not well defined. Most often, the common goal is to have a well-balanced contrast within your frame— where you have bright regions, dark regions, and a good representation of "grey scale" tones in between (Figure 3.24).

High contrast, snappy or punchy, lighting schemes can make for more dramatic or suspenseful imagery, but they also yield more depth to your frame. The interplay of light and shadow across the foreground, middle ground, and background of your shots helps create a layering effect within the set's deep physical space. The irregularity of objects in the frame, including the human face and body, gains a relief or modeling from these pockets of light and dark, which helps them achieve a three-dimensional appearance on the two-dimensional film frame. This type of lighting design is often called **low-key lighting**.

Low contrast, flat or even, lighting schemes can make images seem more open, friendly, or "brighter," but they also yield a flatter, less visually separated frame. Often, the point of low contrast, or **high-key lighting**, is to provide overall even lighting so that all elements of the frame are visible to the viewer. Talk show, news broadcast, and situation

FIGURE 3.24 These abstract images represent a high contrast and a low contrast image.

comedy sets are often lit in a low contrast fashion. This way, the multiple cameras that record the events can all receive proper exposure without the need to continually adjust lighting levels on the set. What you gain in even visibility you lose in dramatic flavor. Additionally, the 2D frame, including all objects in it, will appear flatter and, in the opinion of many, less visually interesting (Figure 3.25).

FIGURE 3.25   Examples of low key and high key lighting schemes.

Contrast

Basic Character Lighting: Three Point Method

How one uses hard light and soft light to gain selective exposure on talent and on set is the fun part of creative lighting for composition. There are innumerable ways for you to place light on your actors, and hopefully, over your career as a filmmaker, you will have the opportunity to experiment with many of them. Starting off on solid ground is useful, however, so we are going to explore the most basic standard in subject illumination—the **three point lighting method**.

The three points actually refer to three distinct jobs that lighting fixtures have when put into particular placements around the film set. Rather than describing the light's properties, these terms define their purposes.

KEY—**Key light** is the one light source around which you build your lighting scheme. It is usually the main provider of illumination to your film set or location. You "key" your other lights (quantity and quality) off this main source. The key light may live anywhere around your subject, but it traditionally is placed 45 degrees (horizontally and vertically) off the axis of the camera's lens and above the height of the talent's head.

FILL—**Fill light** is a light source used to help control contrast. The light energy that it emits "fills in" the shadows often created by the brighter key light. The physical placement of the fill light is on the opposite side of the subject from the key light, roughly 45 degrees (horizontally) off lens axis.

BACK—**Back light** is the light that defines an edge, or halo effect, around the backside of the subject. Because it lives behind the subject (opposite side of the film set from the camera's lens) and provides a light "rim" to the outline of the subject, the back light serves to separate objects from the background and enhance the illusion of depth within the film frame.

The quantity of light from these three lights must be enough to achieve exposure on the scene. Clearly the key light will provide the most illumination. The fill light will contribute varying degrees of additional illumination depending on how low or how high a contrast difference you would like to have (how much or how little shadow). The back light need only apply enough glow to the edge of the subject to "read" or be recorded by the medium (Figures 3.26 and 3.27).

The lighting contrast specific to the human subject is a relationship known as the **contrast ratio** or the ratio of the fill + key side of the face to the fill side of the face. The

FIGURE 3.26 The evolution of the three point lighting method in practice.

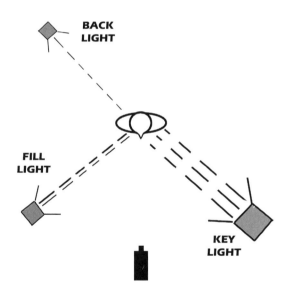

FIGURE 3.27 An overhead schematic of the three point lighting fixture placement.

quantity of light can be measured with a handheld light meter, but you really should develop your "eye" to gauge the relative amounts of light on each side of the face. Even light levels on each side would be a 1:1 lighting ratio and would create a high key scene of even and flat lighting. Differing quantities of light on each side may yield a higher contrast ratio, such as 8:1 or 16:1, and would be described as a low key scene with more deep shadow regions (Figure 3.28).

FIGURE 3.28   Examples of high contrast, "modeled" contrast, and low contrast ratios.

Other contributing factors in the creation of high or low ratios are quality of light (hard or soft) and **angle of incidence**. Hard lights, being more directional, are easier to control, cut, block off, and so on but they also generate the deep shadow associated with a high lighting ratio. Soft light is not so easy to control (where it falls on your subject) but because it tends to wrap around curved surfaces a bit, it can yield lower lighting ratios. The main factor to all this, however, is the light fixture's placement and the resulting angle of incidence or from where the light's rays fall on the surface of the subject.

In fictional narrative cinematography, lighting is generally meant to be **motivated** or generated by some actual source within the reality of the film world. A desk lamp, a TV flicker, a lantern, even the sun itself are all examples of objects that can motivate light on a film set. Then film lights actually generate the recorded light that provides the exposure intensity. Where these motivating light sources exist within the film's world usually dictates where the film lights must be placed as well. If the light is supposed to be coming from a light fixture in the ceiling, then the film light must have an angle of incidence from higher than the subject's head. If someone stands next to a camp fire, then the film firelight effect must have a lower angle of incidence and come from below the subject's head level.

Just as you know that the camera can be placed around the subject along imaginary horizontal or vertical circles, lighting fixtures can be placed in similar ways. When the light is near the recording camera's angle on action, it is called **front lighting**, which tends to flatten out the face and be rather bland in appearance. Depending on the height of the lamp head in this scenario, you may also cause a visible shadow on any surface behind the actor who is front lit. Higher lamp heads from a higher angle of incidence force the shadows down along the floor. Any lights at or below the talent's physical height will throw shadows across the set, which will be visible to the camera lens and is often not visually pleasing. In general, shadows of actors are not welcome on film sets, unless they are being used for creative or thematic purposes.

If we continue our way around the actor and place a light 90 degrees around the circle from the camera to subject axis, it is called **side lighting** and can generate a half-bright half-dark face split along the bridge of the nose. When the light is behind the subject but not exactly opposite to the camera lens it is often called a **kicker** or a **rim light**—highlighting the edges of the hair, shoulders, and sometimes the jaw bone. For the most standard approach to the three-point lighting method, however, you should start with your key light roughly 45 degrees away from camera (left or right) and the fill light about 45 degrees around the other side of camera. Of course, this could all change according to your creative needs or whims.

Most light sources in the real world, and subsequently in the film world, come from above and slightly away. This generally holds true because light that comes from directly above (**top lighting**) will cause the brow ridges on most faces to block the light from the eye sockets. By keeping the eyes of the character in deep shadow you are taking away one very important way for the audience to relate to the character. Conversely, if you light from below, you are creating a rather unnatural lighting effect, as very few lights actually exist below the level of our heads in daily life. As a result of this **underlighting**, the structure of the human face takes on a scary or ghoulish appearance and, therefore, is often used in horror films. If you only illuminate the background of your set and leave your talent's face in darkness (with no fill light) and you expose for the well-lit background, you will create what is called the **silhouette** effect (Figure 3.29).

FIGURE 3.29   Examples of front, side, kicker, top, under, and silhouette lighting.

Basic Character Lighting: Three Point Method

Set and Location Lighting

Creating the silhouette mentioned earlier called for more light on the set or location background and no light on the middle ground talent. This helps us illustrate that placing light on your set (on the walls, furnishings, floor, trees, etc.) or location is often just as important as lighting your talent's face with a scene-appropriate ratio. Certainly you need to add light to your set for general exposure, but placing light on specific areas of the set or location can add to the ambience of the scene, change its tone or mood, and create that additional 3D effect into the deep space of the film set. Light in the middle ground and deep background helps separate those layers of distance discussed earlier. They can also "rim" a subject and help further separate them from the darker background on night shots and so forth.

Any light fixture on your set that actually works and emits light that helps toward exposure and the overall creative lighting design is called a **practical**. Its job is to appear within the frame and provide light to the scene. Most often practical lamps are not bright enough to generate good exposure levels of light so they are usually accent lights that provide points of visual interest around the set or act as motivators for other (off screen) larger film lights that raise exposure levels on the set. Practical lights can also be a good source of motivation for creative color usage, as in "warm" amber fire light, "cool" blue refrigerator interior light, deep red neon light, and so forth.

Color, of course, is another great creative tool for the filmmaker. Beyond the basics of accepted color treatments (blue for moonlight and cooler temperature locations, such as a meat freezer or the Arctic Circle, or amber for warm, safe places, such as a family home or a candle-lit dinner for two) one can use colors to underscore the story's themes or represent a character. Perhaps a person who is jealous or envious of another is always shown wearing green clothes or standing in environments that have a high component of green in them. Maybe a character who feels emotionally distant from others is shown in a pale blue wash until the end of the story when he is united with his loved ones and the overall tone of the shots turns more amber.

These concepts are really just some of the basics of best practices in the discipline, art, science, and craft of film lighting. It is hoped that as you develop your overall skills with shot composition you will be expanding your abilities in the use of creative lighting as well. You cannot have one without the other. As you will grow to understand more and more, everything in filmmaking is related to everything else. Light relates to lens optics, aperture, film/CCD sensitivity, exposure, ratios, color, emotional audience reaction, thematic/character interpretation, and so on and so on. Let us just say that you should always be conscious of how you are lighting your shots. Your lighting and compositional choices need to serve your "story" and not fight against it or leave it seeming bland or incomplete. What you choose to reveal to the audience or hide from them will yield more or less information, more or less understanding, and more or less enjoyment of your project.

Set and Location Lighting

End of Chapter Three Review

1. Understand how to create the illusion of 3D on a 2D image.

2. Horizon line—keep it level and steady.

3. Dutch angle—skews horizontal and vertical lines to create imbalance.

4. Diagonal lines—force perspective to vanishing point and create depth.

5. The depth of film space—foreground/middle ground/background—zones where you stage action and that exist at varying distances from the lens.

6. Object size—large in frame means near and small means far.

7. Atmospherics—great distance is implied via water vapor obscuration.

8. Zoom lenses—wide angle or telephoto—focal lengths capture wide field of view or narrow field of view of the film space.

9. Focus—creatively shifting focus within your film's depth will direct the viewer's eye around your frame and keep them engaged—pull, push, rack, or follow focus.

10. Depth of field—only objects within the DOF will appear to be in acceptable focus to the audience, expand/contract or shift that zone in order to achieve more creative compositions and infuse your shots with energy.

11. Lighting—light is always required to get your basic image to expose—beyond that, use light to separate objects from the background, create compositional areas of interest within the frame, generate 3D illusions via contrast modeling of light and dark regions, set a tone for feelings with high key or low key lighting designs and color usage.

Chapter Four
Putting Your Shots Together: Prethinking the Editing Process

QUESTION: What is "shooting for editing?"

ANSWER: During production, when you are recording all of the visual material for a project, you make sure that your shots cover all of the action from each angle required so that when it comes time to edit the individual shots together, there is enough visual material to show the entire story from the preferred positions of coverage.

It is extremely important to remember that creating and recording all of the shots discussed so far is only one part of the visual storytelling process. While you are shooting, you are in **production**, **but** once you are done recording all of your motion images, the project moves into a phase called **postproduction** or the editing process. What does this mean for you, the camera person or director? It means everything. All the hard work that you do achieving your well-planned shots during production really only serves to enhance the abilities of the people who are doing the postproduction work—the picture and sound editors. They are tasked with assembling all of your shots, whatever they may be, and creating the best documentary, news report, music video, commercial, or feature film that they can. To learn more about the editing process, feel free to review the contents of our companion text, *Grammar of the Edit*.

The responsibility of generating and maintaining the overall visual quality of the work is set on the shoulders of the production team (director, DP, camera operator, etc.). There is a certain degree of psychic ability required for this task because it becomes your job to prethink the needs of the edit team, shoot the appropriate coverage of the material, and deliver the variety of shots that will best show the story. This is called shooting with editing in mind. What will the editor need to cut to at this point? What would the audience like to see next? How can this information be shown at its best? What shot framing will not confuse the viewer? Etc. Etc. Etc.

So far we have only focused on relatively simple shots, single subjects in CU, MS, LS, and so forth. The simple goal of each of these shot types is to present visual information to the audience. The LS shows full action and environment, the MS provides immediately discernible information, and the CU highlights very detailed information.

By recording a variety of these shot types, you provide the editor with more choices. The editor can then decide more freely at what point the viewing audience will desire fresh information and how much or how little information to show. A cut to a new shot type gives that new information. A scene is created when the editor stitches together all of the important information found in each of your shot types and the audience has absorbed all that it can from the material that you originally provided during production.

Matching Your Shots in a Scene

The individual shots you create on set will not live in a void and they will not, most likely, stand alone as independent motion images. In the end, they will work with one another, intercut with one another, so that an entire visual story is told. The shots cut together to make a scene, the scenes cut together to make an ACT, and the acts cut together to make an entire motion picture. Production can span days, weeks, or months of real time, but the resulting images, when edited together, need to appear as though they were all captured at the same exact time with fluid movement and matching actions. Consistency is therefore very important and we have a few ways to help stay aware of the potential glitches (Figure 4.1).

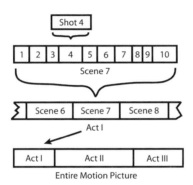

FIGURE 4.1 The evolution of a motion picture's building blocks.

Continuity

When producing a fictional narrative work, and there is a person or event to be recorded, you will most likely run through the action several times, recording each pass from a different angle and with a different shot type in your camera setup. This is called shooting **coverage**. You "cover" the main action from several angles and with several different framings. The ultimate goal, of course, is to make sure that the viewing audience is able to watch the entire action or delivery of dialogue from beginning to end. The editor is allowed to choose when to cut from one shot to the next, and engages the audience by providing them with a variety of coverage.

Having the actors repeat the same action or dialogue from shot to shot requires that you pay attention to **continuity**, which is consistent repetition of movement, action, or dialogue by the talent from one camera setup to the next. Keep in mind that each action and line of dialogue delivery are also repeated within each unique camera setup or shot, recorded as individual units called **takes**. Your goal will be to record as few "takes" as possible to get the action or dialogue correct and usable for the editor, saving time and money, but still getting the coverage you, and the editor, will need. However, continuity is not just making sure an actor moves his hand the same way in each take of each shot. Continuity, on a visual story construction level, involves a much wider range of planning as well.

Continuity of Screen Direction

We all know that the rectangular screen upon which we watch a motion picture is not the place where the actions are actually taking place. Movies can pretty much be shot anywhere and in any direction, yet to the viewing audience, that screen is their one window onto the world of the film. As a result, the filmmakers have a responsibility to the audience to present a knowable world that conforms to some constant, physical world rules such as up, down, left, right, near, far, and so forth such that when the audience watches the motion picture they do not get confused spatially. The horizon line mentioned in Chapter Three is a helpful clue, but there are other ways that you can keep your audience grounded (Figure 4.2).

The frame that confines your selected shot type actually helps keep your audience sure of the location. As we know, the camera occupies the "**fourth wall**," allowing the audience a privileged view of locations and actions within the film's "space." The top, bottom, left, and right edges of the frame therefore become references of direction for the audience. The character looks off frame left—the car drives away and exits frame right. The viewer associates the directional attention of a character or the movement of subjects in the film world to the edges of the frame. It should be clear then that **screen direction**—the left or right movement of a subject—must be maintained from one shot to the next. Figures 4.3 through 4.5 should help illustrate the concept of continuity of screen direction.

The audience member viewing these recorded actions on the screen (Figures 4.3 to 4.5) assumes that there is a larger "film world" beyond the confines of the four edges of the frame. Because this film space exists in its own version of reality, the rules of physical

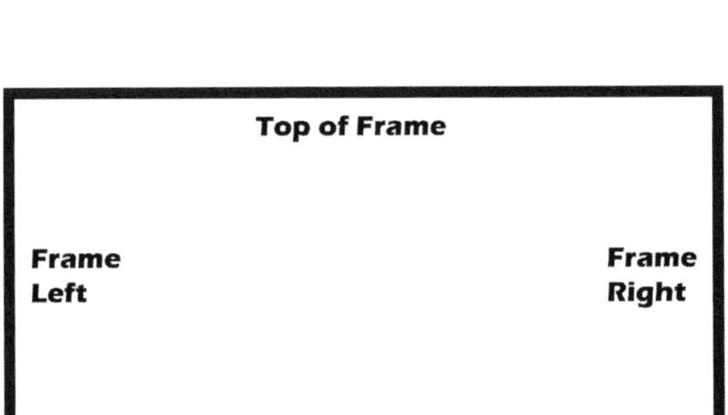

Top of Frame

Frame Left

Frame Right

Bottom of Frame

FIGURE 4.2 The motion picture frame has four edges and corresponding areas of interest: frame left, frame right, top of frame, and bottom of frame.

FIGURE 4.3 Action shows a person walking toward and exiting frame left.

FIGURE 4.4 Holding on empty frame for a bit just after the person has exited.

FIGURE 4.5   Cut to new shot of the same person continuing their walk, but this time they are entering the shot from frame right. Action follows a continuity of screen direction.

movement must be obeyed as in reality—if a person moves away to the left they must keep moving away to the left until we see some change in the movement happen on screen. That is, if during a shot, a person walks out of frame left, you could assume a continuance of movement in that direction until the next shot picks up their ongoing journey. The character's leftward motion, however, dictates that in this new shot they would have to be entering from frame right in order to maintain that direction of leftward movement within the film's space.

Continuity of Screen Direction

The Line—Basis for Screen Direction

Not all screen direction is based on large, physical movements. A good deal of important narrative information and spatial relationship data can be discerned by the viewing audience just through their observation of the directions of **attention**. Most often, each subject within the film space pays attention to some other subject or object within the same film space. The child looks after a lost balloon (Figure 4.6)—the dog looks at the burglar (Figure 4.7)—the hungry man looks at the pie in the baker's window (Figure 4.8). The

FIGURE 4.6   The child's attention follows the ascending balloon. A line is created.

FIGURE 4.7   The dog looks in the direction of the intruder. A line is created.

audience is keen on observing these attentions and, as a result, uses these connections between people and people, people and objects, and so on to establish **lines of direction**, which are also called **sight lines**. Good filmmakers know that an audience desires these connections, wants to follow these lines of attention, and uses this phenomenon to help establish narrative meaning and shot composition and to reinforce spatial relationships within the film space.

FIGURE 4.8 The hungry man eyes the baker's fresh pie. A line is created.

The Line—Basis for Screen Direction

The Imaginary Line—The 180 Degree Rule

The lines of attention need to be understood, established, and respected by the production team. As the audience relies upon these to receive and maintain spatial cues, it is very important that they remain consistent throughout the editing of a scene. To help maintain lines of attention and screen direction from shot to shot there is a popular filmmaker's concept known by several names: **180 degree line**, **imaginary line**, **action line**, or **axis of action**. As some of the names imply, it is an imaginary line drawn through the shooting location, roughly where all of the main action occurs, and it is established by tracing the sight line of the talent within the shot (Figure 4.9).

This concept's other name, the **180 degree rule**, will surely help clarify how this all works the way it does and why it is so important. Much like we discussed the horizontal camera angle circling around your stationary subject back in Chapter Two, we will once again imagine that your subject(s) is at the center of a large circle. For your first shot, the camera is once again positioned at the outer ring of the circle facing in toward the center where your action is occurring. Now superimpose in your mind the action line cutting across the diameter of the circle from frame left to frame right (Figure 4.10).

Once you have established this first line, it pretty much stays locked in place, but there are ways to alter it while shooting coverage. Of course, to get other shots of your subjects you will have to move the camera around the film space, but now you will have to respect this initial axis of action. The line has cut an arc out of the imaginary circle that is 180 degrees around from side to side. Your camera must now operate within that 180 degree arc when you set up for your new camera angles and coverage shots (Figure 4.11).

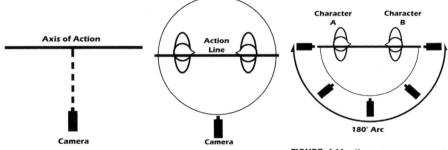

FIGURE 4.9 Overhead of 180 degree line along the axis of action.

FIGURE 4.10 Bird's-eye view of the action line.

FIGURE 4.11 Keep your camera setups within the 180 degree arc on the near side of the established action line.

The first shot establishes frame left and frame right and also establishes the lines of attention throughout the film space. Character A is talking with character B. A is sitting frame left and his sight lines are pointing frame left to frame right. B is sitting frame right (receiving A's attention) and is looking back at A (sending sight lines from frame right to frame left). When you frame your shot for a single CU of A you would need to maintain screen direction and continuity. A is still frame left with attention pointing frame right (even though B is no longer physically visible within the frame). Cutting back to B in her CU would necessitate a similar treatment. B is framed toward the right, looking out frame left. The series of shots and overhead diagrams in Figure 4.12 should help solidify this practice.

The Imaginary Line—The 180 Degree Rule

FIGURE 4.12   Respecting the imaginary line and staying within the 180 degree arc will result in correct continuity of screen direction across the shots of this dialogue scene.

"Jumping the Line"

It does happen from time to time, but most filmmakers do not notice it until they get into the editing process. To "**jump the line**" or "**cross the line**" means that you placed the camera on the opposite side of the action line and recorded coverage shots from the wrong side of the 180 degree arc—effectively reversing the established directions of left and right and inverting the film space on the unaware viewer. In the series of shots shown in Figure 4.13, the first two are repeated from our example given earlier, but the third shot is taken, by mistake, from the far side of the arc. The result is a nice

FIGURE 4.13 Only when edited together does one see the incorrect screen direction of character B's attention in the close-up. The camera had jumped the axis of action.

CU of character B, but the real mistake is not apparent until the three shots are edited together. B's screen direction and line of attention are reversed and therefore the cuts make no sense because it now appears that both A and B are sitting in the same fashion looking off frame right, not looking back and forth at one another as established in the wider two shot.

Crossing the line is acceptable under certain circumstances, which are explored in more detail in Chapter Six. For now, just think of how you would have to cover a couple slow dancing cheek to cheek on a dance floor. You would have one face on one side of a head and the other face on the opposite side, with the axis of action cutting through each. In order to see both faces, you would have to cross the line to set up your shot. As you may have picked up by now, there are very few absolutes when it comes to the guidelines and "rules" presented in this text. Remember, if you have creative reasons to execute a certain shot or group of shots a certain way, then do it, even if it flies in the face of convention.

"Jumping the Line"

The 30 Degree Rule

Grounded in the execution of the 180 degree rule is another important guideline called the **30 degree rule**. Simply put, when you are seeking various angles on action for a variety of shot types within your 180 degree arc, you should ideally move the camera at least 30 degrees around the semicircle before you begin to frame up a new shot of the same subject. The angle of view or perspective on the same subjects is considered "different enough" when the camera is moved away from the previous setup by at least 30 degrees. Because each shot or view of the action is supposed to show new information to the audience, it makes sense that you would not wish to create two separate coverage shots that are too similar to one another. Following this 30 degree rule can help prevent this similarity in repeated shots when the edit process is underway. This will avoid what is known as a **jump cut**—two shots with similar framing of the same object cut together causing a visual jump in either space or time within the film's world (Figures 4.14 and 4.15).

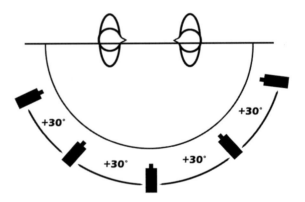

FIGURE 4.14   A 180 degree arc from the action line broken down into 30 degree slices.

FIGURE 4.15   The same subjects as seen through the camera at five 30 degree slices around the 180 degree arc. This maintains the action line and achieves a new angle on action appropriate for the edit.

The 30 Degree Rule

Reciprocating Imagery

Our recent example of shots cutting from a wider two-shot to two singles in a medium close-up serves well to illustrate our next point. Whenever you shoot one type of shot to cover one character in a scene you should create the exact same corresponding frame for the other character in the scene. They call this **matching shots** or **reciprocating imagery** (Figure 4.16).

Tradition holds that an editor might normally show a scene from the outside in, where the shots of the action start off wider to show environment and characters and then, as the action progresses, cut together tighter and closer shots in order to show more intimate detail by the end. Each new camera setup with new framing should match for object size and object placement. Of course, you may have to make allowances for actual subject size, hairstyle, hat, or other accessories that may require slightly different framing. Your main goal, however, will be to provide the editor with equal numbers of shots and matching framing for each character. When it comes time to cut, he or she can progress along shot size or type from one character to the next.

The same can be said for the camera angle itself. Generally speaking, when you cover two separate characters with single shots from the same scene, you should take care to match the camera height, camera lens angle (tilted up or down or neutral), and overall camera

FIGURE 4.16 Shooting matching shots for medium close-up coverage is best. Providing an editor with an MCU of one character but only a BCU of the other may cause issues during the edit. The shot types do not match.

angle on action. Of course, because you must take your storytelling needs into account, not every aspect may match exactly. The overall camera angle on action, though, is tied in with the 180 degree rule and the associated geometry really helps keep everything organized. If you shoot character A from a 45 degree angle around your 180 degree arc, then you should swing the camera around to the other end of your arc and shoot character B from a corresponding 45 degree angle. Provided that you keep the same camera height and lens focal length, you should be able to easily generate the reciprocating image of the second character that matches the framing of the first shot (Figures 4.17 and 4.18).

When two subjects appear in the same frame, the same matching shot rules apply. For example, the **over-the-shoulder** shot allows the audience to keep track of the physical placement of each character in the scene. Lines of attention and screen direction are still required to maintain spatial relations. When you establish a frame that favors character A's face, you include a portion of the backside of character B's head and shoulder.

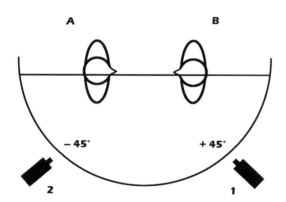

FIGURE 4.17   Camera setup 1 records MS of character A from 45 degrees on the arc. Camera setup 2 records MS of character B from −45 degrees on the opposite side of the same arc.

Reciprocating Imagery

FIGURE 4.18   The resulting matching MS shots of characters A and B.

For consistency in editing purposes, the reverse shot, favoring character B's face, must also be recorded. The audience will often expect that reverse shot to be matching in subject size, subject composition, camera height, angle on action, and so forth, unless you are providing purposefully altered framing for storytelling reasons. When cutting from one OTS to another, any differences in these image factors will be very apparent and the mismatch will cause your audience, perhaps just on a subconscious level, to have an unfavorable reaction to the scene (Figures 4.19 and 4.20).

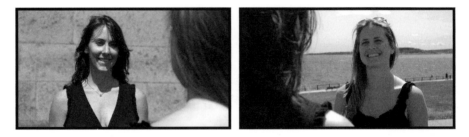

FIGURE 4.19   Matching over-the-shoulder shots for characters A and B.

FIGURE 4.20   Mismatching over-the-shoulder shots for characters A and B. Note how the subjects framing, size, and angle are not consistent.

Eye-Line Match

Another important notion associated with shooting for editing is the concept of **eye-line match**. This takes the line of attention or sight line from one shot and ties it directly with an object in a new shot after a transition. Eye-line match usually involves a character isolated within a frame (perhaps illustrated most easily with an MS or an MCU shot) when their attention is directed somewhere outside the four edges of that frame. The audience traces an imaginary line from the character's eyes to the edge of the frame where they are looking.

The filmmaker, most often, is then obliged to have to show the audience what the character is looking at. The next shot should be that object of interest revealed to the audience. And it's not just revealed in some arbitrary shot. It should be shot from a similar direction, angle, and height that closely match what the perspective would be from the vantage point of the character observing the object in the first shot. This does not have to be a direct, subjective POV shot, but it does have to maintain and respect the eye-line established with the observing character so that the audience feels adequately informed that they, too, are seeing the same object as the character in the film.

Eye-line match is a "setup and then payoff" scenario maker. The first shot sets up an expectation and then the second shot fulfills that expectation. The important thing is to frame the second shot from a corresponding vantage point so that the illusion of connection and character association is made by the audience (Figure 4.21).

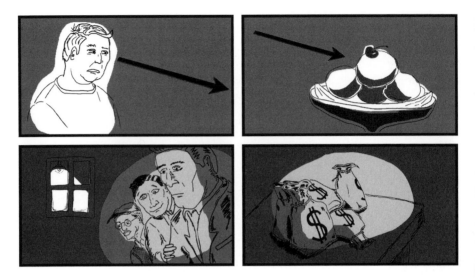

FIGURE 4.21 The first shot sets up the subject and the eye-line of interest. The second shot, presented from a correspondingly subjective viewpoint, reveals the object of interest.

End of Chapter Four Review

1. The shots you create must be edited together so plan for that process.
2. Watch for continuity of action in performance.
3. Maintain continuity of screen direction from one shot to another.
4. Let the line of attention connect objects for the audience.
5. Use sight lines and the action line to maintain proper screen direction while shooting coverage for a scene.
6. Move the camera at least 30 degrees (or more) around your shooting arc and change your focal length so no two shots of coverage seem to come from the same angle on action.
7. Always match your shots for framing, angle, focal length, and so on when shooting a multicharacter scene, unless you have a creative motivation to do otherwise.
8. An eye-line match keeps your audience informed and grounded. Expectations are set up in one shot and paid off in the next.

Chapter Five
Dynamic Shots — Talent and Camera in Motion

QUESTION: How do you keep the camera steady?

ANSWER: Any way you can.

The answer to this question is a bit glib, but it clearly illustrates the importance of maintaining a steady image. What good would it do to prepare a well-composed shot only to have its image blurred or confused by an unstable camera? Not much good at all. The same would go for talent that suddenly moved around your shot, compromising your carefully planned composition and depth of field. Now this does not mean that all shots need to be static, but it does drive home the point that your movements should be well planned, well executed, and even designed as part of the overall "character" or "mood" of your motion picture.

We began our exploration of the grammar of the shot with very simple, single subject, static shots. Static means no movement, but because we are shooting motion pictures it will be a good idea to incorporate more movement into the shots and scenes. Next, with a camera still "locked-off" we introduced talent movement: people exiting or entering the frame and so forth. Let us briefly touch on this topic of talent movement while we are at this point.

Blocking Talent

Remember that humans respond well to brightness, color, and movement. The movement of talent, then, within the static frame is a great way to infuse your shot with visual energy. The term **staging** is often used to describe the physical placement of subjects on the film set and within the confines of the recorded frame. The term **blocking** is often used to describe the physical movement of subjects on the film set and within the confines of the same frame. Creating interesting blocking can engage the viewer's eye and keep them involved in the current image and therefore in the story. Talent blocking across the screen (left to right or vice versa) helps reinforce space and direction. Talent blocking deep into the set or location adds to the illusion of a three-dimensional film frame (Figure 5.1).

Static shots and stationary talent can have energy and power all their own. It depends on the type of motion picture project that you are creating. Talent movement, when blocked creatively, will add energy to your shots. In some schools of film theory, even the direction of movement can have meaning within the narrative. As an example, in an American frontier story, characters on a long journey to the territories may always have a screen right to screen left movement, perhaps implying that the right is East and the left is West. Maybe a character is always moving from the foreground of a shot into the background—perhaps this means that he is running away or is too mysterious to be captured up close within the frame for very long.

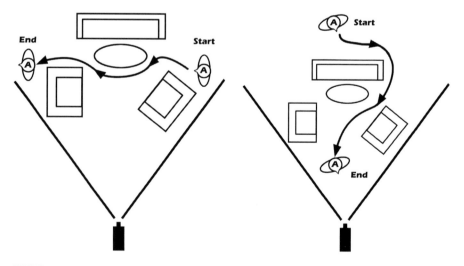

FIGURE 5.1 Talent blocking may be across the frame, deep into the frame, or both.

Camera in Motion

If having your talent move within a static frame puts energy into your shot, then imagine what will happen once you start moving the camera while recording your images. Since the camera becomes the view point of privilege for your audience, a moving camera will really take them on a ride. Gauging just the right kind and amount of movement is one of your creative and technical decisions—too little could be just distracting and too much could be plain confusing. In order to figure this out, it would be helpful if we explored the many ways in which the camera can move.

Handheld

Perhaps the best place to begin a discussion of camera movement is with the most challenging—going **handheld**. You may find it convenient to hold a smaller camera in your hand, but just because it is a readily available mode of shooting does not mean that it is appropriate and it certainly does not mean it is easy to do well. The first factor involved is a technical one: what camera you are going to use to shoot your project. Modern digital video technologies have allowed for cameras to be quite small and quite capable; they can weigh a few ounces to just a few pounds. If you are working on an emulsion film motion picture, the nature of the medium requires much heavier and much bulkier camera equipment—often weighing in at 20 to 50 pounds or more. This is not necessarily conducive to handheld shooting, although they do have specially designed cameras for just such a purpose.

The smaller, more lightweight handheld camera is simultaneously a blessing and a curse. It allows for easy movement, but that often leads to too much movement. Having and using a tripod is always encouraged, especially if you are new to shooting motion pictures. Remember, everything you do with your shots should have a purpose and choosing to shoot handheld should not come about because you lack the appropriate **camera support**, but rather because you know that your story will benefit from the kinetic energy that a well-controlled handheld camera can bring to a project. Perhaps it would be best to compile a brief list of advantages and disadvantages for the handheld camera option.

Advantages

- Easy to readjust framing on the fly
- Creates sense of personal immediacy within the scene (subjective POV)
- Allows operator to move freely around the set or location
- Imbues shots with energy of motion

Disadvantages

- Easily becomes too shaky or causes swaying on the horizon line
- Difficult to manage focus
- Difficult to cut with static camera shots
- Too subjective, may be inappropriate for neutral voice of the motion picture
- Generally limits focal length usage to wider fields of view because the more environment visible within the frame, the more "stable" the image will appear

Pan and Tilt

Pan and **tilt** refer to the horizontal and vertical repositioning of the camera lens. A pan (or panoramic shot) keeps the camera anchored to the center of an imaginary circle but rotates or swivels the camera lens horizontally such that it views the outside of the circle in an arcing motion. Pan shots are often referred to as "sweeping" because they can encompass large swaths of wide open landscape with only a few degrees of sweep along the arc of the panning circle (see Figure 5.2). A tilt rotates or swivels the camera's lens along a vertical axis during the recording of a shot. If a balloon floats out of a child's hand and drifts up to the clouds, the shot can start with the lens pointing down toward the ground and end tilting up toward the sky in order to follow the path of the balloon (see Figure 5.3).

There is also a combination shot that combines a pan with a tilt where the camera lens is simultaneously panned across the film space and tilted up or, conversely, the camera is tilted down while panning across. Either way this results in a diagonal motion through the film space in front of the camera. An example could be two people who are about to enter a large building—as they pause (frame left) to look at the imposing façade (currently out of the frame), the camera sweeps up and across the location to the right in order to end the shot on the building itself. An upward diagonal **tilt–pan** has been executed to cover both the people and the building.

The action of a pan or a tilt is actually an unnatural experience for the human visual system. Our eyes and brains do not make smooth pans or tilts while viewing our surroundings. Instead, the eye travels along the space locking onto points of interest, registering with the brain, and then shooting along quickly to the next point of interest. It becomes a very rapid series of starts, stops, starts, stops with the resulting illusion that

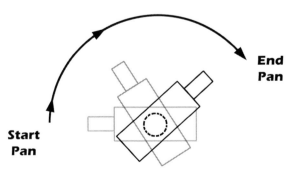

FIGURE 5.2 Overhead of camera panning horizontally during a shot.

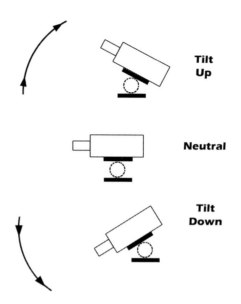

FIGURE 5.3 Profile view of camera tilting from neutral position to up or down positions.

we have panned along the environment or tilted our eyes up the building or mountainside. Because a motion picture camera lens is not as selective, everything that it "sees" throughout the duration of the pan or tilt gets equal treatment. The smooth execution of a pan or tilt and the speed of that execution directly impact how the human audience receives the information within the movement of the shot.

To help the audience accept the camera's panning or tilting movement, it is often good to motivate the move. In our examples so far we have provided these motivations. The upward movement of the lost balloon motivates the camera to follow the action tilting up toward the sky. The audience would like to see what happens to the balloon so they would naturally wish to follow its motion upward. Then we have the two characters who stop and stare up at the imposing structure of the building. Their eye-line from frame left across to upper frame right motivates the diagonal camera tilt–pan to **reveal** the façade of the building. The camera fulfills the expectation in one shot by showing the audience the object of the characters' interest.

Remember that an audience member often places him- or herself in the position of your camera—identifying with the role of that observer. When the camera moves, it then takes on a sort of intelligence, following action or seeking information or resolution. Motivating your camera moves (pans and tilts especially) helps keep the flow going. There are times, however, when you creatively have no visible motivating action for the camera to follow on a pan or a tilt. Perhaps you wish to shoot a long, slow pan of photographs depicting several generations of a family or maybe there are many different pairs of shoes in the front hallway of a home you would like to shoot—there is no motivating motion of these subjects, but the camera, when moved slowly, can still record the images and not disturb the audience. The slow speed of the camera's progression is a great way to help smooth over the panning or tilting action.

Pan and Tilt

Shooting the Pan and the Tilt

There is a preferred method to accomplishing a good pan or a good tilt shot. When you first start out operating a camera on pans and tilts they should have three components: the **start frame**, the **camera movement**, and the **end frame**. A pan or tilt composed of all three elements will be able to be edited into your scene more easily than if you had just movement alone.

The Start Frame

Almost every pan or tilt should begin on a static frame, especially when you are just starting out as a camera operator. Your start frame is a well-composed still shot that could stand alone as a good static image. It is from this start frame that the subject that motivates the pan or tilt begins its action. Keep the camera still, let the action begin, and then begin the camera's panning or tilting. We do not discuss editing much in this text, but a quick word to the wise: cutting on movement, either into a shot already in motion or out of a shot once in motion, is a visually dangerous thing to do and often looks bad. Your editor will thank you when you begin your pan or tilt shot with several seconds of static start frame.

The Camera Movement

Once the subject's motion has begun, your camera movement also begins. The camera's motion should ideally be smooth and steady and actually "lead" the movement of the subject. By this we mean that proper headroom, look room, and pictorial composition should be maintained throughout the life of the pan or tilt action. Any individual frame extracted from the shot during the camera movement phase would be able to stand on its own as a well-composed still image. Because the camera is leading the subject's progress, the camera would naturally reach the end of its horizontal or vertical arc prior to the subject completing its movement.

The End Frame

As the camera has already come to a rest before the subject completes the movement, the end frame has been reached successfully. This end frame should, once again, be a well-composed static shot that can complete the pan or tilt action in a visually compelling fashion. You would linger on this end frame, recording several seconds of it while there is no camera movement. The editor now has a steady, locked-off frame to cut out from at the end of your pan or tilt.

As you become a more experienced filmmaker and camera operator, you will be in a better place to experiment with a moving camera on pan/tilt shots without static frames at the head and the tail, especially if they cover a series of very fast action shots. The easiest test is to shoot two versions of the same pan or tilt actions, the shots just before and the shots just after, and then edit each test together. Most often the static start and end frames will help during the edit process.

Shooting the Pan and the Tilt

Equipment Used to Move the Camera

Pan and tilt shots require no equipment to be accomplished with some degree of success. They can be done with a handheld camera. One of the problems inherent to using a handheld camera is the lack of consistently steady control over the movements. No matter how steady you try to make your hands and arms, the camera, especially the smaller, lightweight video cameras, pick up on each step, bump, and even breath. And no matter what you think may be a cool or popular style of crazy camera movement, nothing can take the place of smooth, steady shots that engage the audience rather than alienating them. It is almost always advisable to use some sort of camera support that will not only steady the camera, but allow it to do more well-controlled, precise movements.

Tripod

To begin with, the camera should always have a companion piece of support equipment to keep it stable and level. The **tripod** is the ideal tool to do this job. Tripods come in different sizes and weights depending on the camera that needs to be supported but they all have three legs. The three-leg design allows for solid balance and leveling on most surfaces. You attach the camera to what is called the **tripod head**. On most models, the tripod head is designed to provide pan and tilt movements—thus it is often called a **pan and tilt head**. Attached to the head is an armature that allows you, through the use of torque, to execute rather smooth pan and tilt movements by grabbing this arm and swiveling the tripod head on either a horizontal or a vertical axis. This stick is called the **pan handle**. Advanced tripod heads for professional motion picture work are called **geared heads** and use two wheels to pivot the camera through pans and tilts and there is no pan handle per se.

A level, locked-off tripod allows you to record extremely stable simple static shots. A tripod with the pan lock loosened allows for very smooth and level horizontal pans. The pan lock engaged and the tilt lock loosened allow for very accurate tilting movements up and down without any drifting to the left or right. One would have to have both pan and tilt locks disengaged in order to maneuver the tripod head to execute a smooth and stable diagonal pan–tilt. Tripods will generally sit directly upon the floor or the ground, and a device called a **spreader** (that attaches to all three legs from the center) keeps them from spreading too far apart and dropping the camera too low to the ground. Tripods are also commonly referred to as **support**, **legs,** or **sticks**.

Tripod

Dolly

The original motion picture cameras had a hand-cranked film transport mechanism, which meant that one hand (often the right) of the camera operator was constantly engaged in turning the crank during the actual recording of the shot. The camera was mounted on a tripod and the entire apparatus did not move during the shooting. The desire for camera movement quickly led to experiments where the camera and tripod were attached to a four-wheeled cart. The operator would stand on a platform, cranking the camera, and other crew members (now called **grips**) would push or pull the entire apparatus around the film set or location. This, in essence, evolved into the modern-day film **dolly**.

At their roots, all dollies are wheeled platforms. Some have three wheels, some have four wheels, and some have many small ball-bearing wheels like those on a skateboard. Many dollies have thick rubber or air-filled wheels that allow it to be pushed or pulled around relatively flat surfaces like a gymnasium floor or along the tiled hallway of a school building. Other dollies have grooved, hard rubber wheels that fit on tracks on the ground. These tracks (or rail) are like small railroad tracks and come in straight or curved sections and you can assemble different lengths to create a path for the dolly to follow (Figure 5.4).

Each of these different dolly types also has different ways to mount the camera to them. Some simple ones are just flat beds that let the tripod and the operator sit on top. Others have a built-in pedestal that can be raised or lowered via hydraulics. Still others have a **boom arm** that sits atop the pedestal and the camera and head are mounted to the end of the boom, allowing for wheeled movement and camera height and angle changes all at the same time.

The most basic job of the dolly is to smoothly transport the camera across short distances. As with most occasions of operating a motion picture camera, you would want the dolly, whether it is on the floor or on tracks, to run through its course as smoothly as possible. The slower the movement of the camera across space, the more visible every little bump will be. The faster the movement the easier it is to hide bumps, but the more difficult it becomes to capture meaningful visual information in your shot. Just as the pan and tilt had three components, so too does a dolly move have the static start frame, the camera dolly movement, and finally the static end frame. Let us take a look at the two major movements of direction that can be accomplished with a dolly.

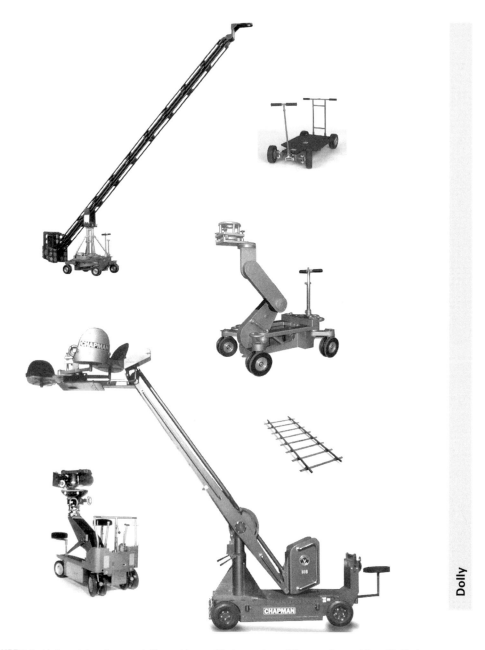

FIGURE 5.4   Various styles of camera dollies and booms. (Photos courtesy of Chapman-Leonard, Inc., J.L. Fischer, Inc., Matthews Studio Equipment.)

Dolly

Crab

Much like a crab on the seashore walks sideways, a dolly can be pushed left or right parallel to the action being recorded. In this case, however, even though the dolly is physically moving parallel to the subjects, the camera is facing the action in a perpendicular fashion. Traditionally, during the **crab dolly**, the camera moves at the same pace as the walking talent. Picture a person walking down the sidewalk of their urban neighborhood greeting the many people he encounters along the way. The camera and dolly would be set in the street and pushed along the street at the same pace as the actor as he progresses down the sidewalk. Parked cars may make up the foreground, the man and the neighbors would make up the middle ground, and the store fronts and stoops of the apartment buildings would make up the background (see Figure 5.5).

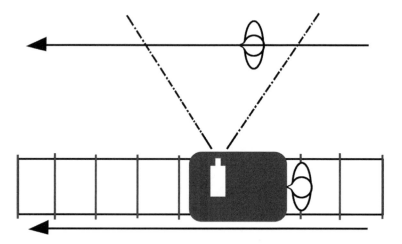

FIGURE 5.5 Although the crab dolly rides parallel to the action's direction, the camera lens is actually perpendicular to the movement.

Truck

If you need to push the camera into the set or in toward a subject being recorded, then you are "**trucking in**." If you need to pull the camera out away from the set or the subject being recorded, then you are "**trucking out**." These movements may also be referred to as **tracking in** and **tracking out**. This type of dolly move usually entails that the dolly and the camera are pointing in the same direction. The one axis glides deep into the set or out of the set in a straight line.

When done slowly, you achieve a barely noticeable change in shot type: a long shot becomes a medium shot and a medium shot ends as a close-up. This is a way to alter framing or shot type without having to perform a cut during the edit process. You basically alter the framing and composition of the shot over space and time during the recording of the shot. Unlike a zoom, which alters magnification and perspective on objects, this movement appears much more natural to an audience member as the moving camera lens acts like our own visual system and maintains perspective on the changing field of view. When done slowly enough, the dolly movement is barely apparent to the consciousness of the viewer—things have just changed somehow but no one "saw" how. This trick is also achievable with a very slow zoom where the framing and perspective changes are too subtle to be overtly observed (Figure 5.6).

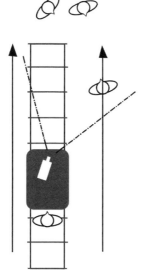

Truck

FIGURE 5.6 Overhead showing the dolly trucking in to the set along the tracks.

One can certainly combine several of these movements discussed so far in order to create a more complex shot that is sometimes called a developing shot. You could have talent move through a set as the camera dollies along the ground to follow the action and have the camera boom up the pedestal to alter the lens height during the take. A focal length change could even be introduced during a developing shot. The movement of the dolly and the possible pan or tilt can help disguise the zoom factor as the unnatural focal length change occurs. It can be very visually interesting to the audience but each element has to be accomplished correctly or all these moves only serve to befuddle the action and confuse the viewer.

We have not mentioned it during any of this movement discussion, but it should be made apparent once more that **focus** is going to be a major concern of any camera operator engaged in these sorts of movement shots. Camera to subject distances will change where focus falls on the set and it is the job of the camera assistant and camera operator to keep these consistent throughout the duration of the shot. This can become quite difficult and requires a great deal of preparation and organization on the part of both talent and crew. It is often best to run through the action for several rehearsals so that talent, camera operator, camera assistant, and dolly grip all understand what the timing of the shot is going to be like. These complex developing shots that involve talent movement, camera movement, focus changes, and possible focal length changes can eat up a lot of time on set so be careful with your scheduling on that shoot day.

Steadicam

For the most part, dollies are limited in the direction of their movements (left, right, in, out). Handheld camera work can be liberating but you constantly run the risks of bad framing, bad focus, and too much shaky movement. Luckily, a device called the Steadicam was invented in the 1970s that allows a camera to be mounted to a spring arm that mounts onto a body harness that is worn by a walking camera operator. This clever device makes it possible for a camera to achieve dolly-like smoothness as it is maneuvered on foot with a super-steady handheld immediacy. Focal length and focus are controlled remotely by an assistant, but composition and movement are controlled by the operator wearing the vest harness. Because the camera is freed from having to follow dolly tracks, the Steadicam allows for rather long and intricate tracking shots as talent moves into and out of sets or locations, up or down stairways, and over rough terrain.

Cranes and Such

Sometimes your motion picture project calls for a grand, sweeping shot of an exterior location. A camera at ground level, regardless of how wide your lens, just cannot encompass as broad a section of your film space as you would like to see. This is where the use of **cranes** comes in. Much like large cranes allow construction equipment to work up high, cranes employed for film use allow the camera to work up high. There are many different types and sizes of cranes, but the general idea is to lift the camera (and often the camera operator as well) up in the air over the set or location to achieve a very high angle view down on the action. Many crane-like devices called **jibs** also have the ability to "boom" the camera from ground level up to higher elevations during the actual recording of the shot. This movement, although not a natural move, is fluid and graceful and has become accepted by viewing audiences over time. Crane shots will help you show a lot of information from a high angle or even a bird's-eye view and can add mobility that energizes the shot for the viewer. You will often see crane or jib shots used as establishing shots to open a scene or summation shots that close out a scene.

End of Chapter Five Review

1. Blocking plans out the movement of your talent around the set.

2. A handheld camera should serve a narrative purpose. Beware of shaky cam syndrome and questionable focus.

3. Horizontal pans and vertical tilts should ideally begin with a static start frame, move smoothly through the camera motion, and finish on a well-composed static end frame.

4. The tripod is the best way to secure smooth, level, stable shots that will cut together.

5. A wheeled dolly, whether on tracks or just the floor, helps achieve smooth gliding camera shots in either crab mode or trucking mode.

6. The Steadicam device combines the best qualities of smooth dolly work with the ease of movement of handheld photography.

7. Cranes, booms, and jib arms help you get sweeping upward or downward moves that add large areas of information and a sense of grandeur to your shots.

Chapter Six
Working Practices and General Guidelines

QUESTION: How do you get to be a good camera operator?

ANSWER: Shoot. Shoot. Shoot some more.

So far we have built up our understanding of the grammar of the shot from the rather basic to the more complex. You should be more familiar with the types of shots, guidelines covering framing and composition, lens choices, prethinking the editor's needs, and camera movement. The grammar you are learning and putting into practice is a well-established and proven set of principles that will enable your audience to understand your visual intentions, but in filmmaking, as with any discipline or craft, there are many different ways of approaching the material, finding solutions to the challenges, and, ultimately, creating your finished work. Although not an exhaustive list by any means, the content of this chapter is designed to help flesh out the rules of film language by offering general guidelines that will enhance your visual presentation and could possibly prevent some headaches down the road.

Communicating with Talent

As a camera operator, there will be many occasions when you will need to interact with on-camera talent. This may hold especially true when you are working on your own projects, because small budgets usually mean smaller crews. Smaller crews mean fewer people to do more work. Because the camera operator is usually in the thick of the action and is responsible for good framing and focus, it makes sense for him or her to help direct the blocking and movement of the talent. This does not mean that you are directing the project (although you may also be the actual director), but rather you are helping the talent understand the limitations of your framing of the shot—how much room do they have to look, move, gesticulate, and so on before they encounter the edges of the frame you have established for the shot.

When you do communicate with the talent, try to keep the interaction brief, clear, and professional. Above all, you should be using language that makes sense to them. Remember that as you sit behind the camera facing the talent, they are facing you and your worlds' directions are mirrored. What is to their right will be to your left and vice versa. In order to keep things simple, provide stage directions that fit with the talent's alignment to the set or location. If you need them to slide over to your frame left a bit more, say something like "Please slide to your right by an inch or two." This method makes it immediately clear in their mind in what direction they are to move and by how much (Figure 6.1).

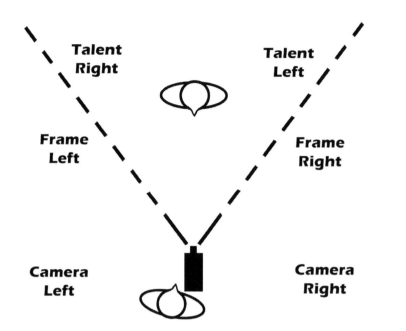

FIGURE 6.1   The camera's frame left and frame right are rarely stage left and stage right for the talent. Speak in their terms and directions will be easy to follow.

Communicating with Talent

Shooting a Big Close-Up or Extreme Close-Up

If you need to shoot a big close-up or an extreme close-up of a human face or hands, be very clear with your talent exactly how tight the framing really is. This enables them to better judge the limitations of their possible on-camera movements for such a tight shot. A big close-up is going to be achieved either through a very close camera proximity to talent or via a rather long focal length lens on a camera slightly farther away. In either case, the resulting frame represents a magnification of the person's face or hands and therefore the entire screen will be filled with that information.

With such extreme magnification, the slightest movements of the talent can "break frame" (move beyond the edges of the established tight frame), alter good composition to bad, change critical focus within the depth of field, and so forth. Your goal would be to have talent move as little as possible on these very close shots. If action is called for, be very precise with how little movement is really required and communicate that clearly to the talent. You may even choose to show them physically what you need by doing it yourself.

There is an old expression concerning an actor's performance that says "less is more." Slow, subtle movements and minor changes in facial expressions yield more visual impact in the close-up shots and help deliver a more significant performance. In the

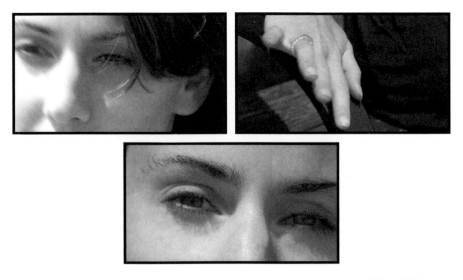

FIGURE 6.2   It is easy to "break frame" or lose focus when dealing with human subjects in BCU and XCU shots.

end, when you are planning your shots for coverage, incorporate big close-up and extreme close-up shots of "details" with discretion. If they fit your overall visual style for the project, have a place in the narrative, and provide important details to the audience, then they will fit in with your other shot types. If not, they have the potential to be too "big" and run the risk of standing out as visual anomalies within your total project.

Documentaries involving mainly "**talking head**" interview close-up shots are the clear exception and projects of this kind, such as portraits of individuals, will call on you to shoot long takes of faces in MS, MCU, CU, and BCU even when they are not speaking. Such intimate close-up detail of the human face in these documentaries allows the audience to really investigate the features of the individual, see into their eyes, and get a feel for who the person is.

Shooting a Big Close-Up or Extreme Close-Up

Ensure an Eye Light

We do not discuss film lighting very much in this book, but it is such a hugely important part of motion image capture that you should be studying lighting as much as possible throughout your career. Of course, we cannot incorporate all of the scientific, thematic, and artistic importance of light and lighting into this presentation so we will include this significant practice that can make a big difference in how your MS and CU shots are received by your viewing audience—the **eye light**.

It has been a long-standing practice in portraiture (painting, still photography, motion pictures) to include what some people call the "life light" or "eye twinkle" in your subject's eyes. This point of light visible in the talent's eyes causes a twinkle and helps draw your audience into looking more closely at the face and eyes of the character. Having light reflected off the eyes implies the spark of life. Having no eye light can imply that the character is dark, evil, duplicitous, is no longer living, or, as in a horror film, might be a vampire or robot.

Thanks to the moist surface and curvature of the human eye, any light source in front of the talent will reflect off the eye and be recorded in the image. A medium shot is

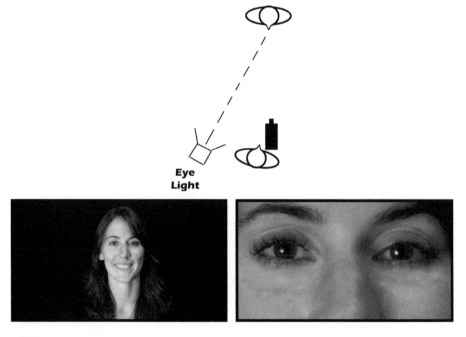

FIGURE 6.3 A light source placed along the axis of the lens will help generate an eye light on the recorded image.

about the most distant shot that may have the small point of light in the eye be "read" or visible on the frame. Anything in the family of close-up shots should have some light source set up near the axis of the lens for giving your talent the eye light unless you are withholding the "life light" for creative purposes.

Whether you are using a point source, a soft source, a bounce, or the sun, the important thing is to make sure that the reflection in the eye shows the light source coming from the correct direction of other known light sources in the film world. Because most lighting fixtures in reality and in film worlds are above the head of the people, the reflection would be in the middle to the top hemisphere of the human eye as seen through the camera's lens. In certain instances, as with a desk lamp, computer screen, or water reflection, the eye's twinkle light may come from below and be visible in the bottom half of the eye. In the end, because the eyes are so important, it is almost always a good idea to give them as much attention as you can in all your shots, even just for reasons of good exposure (Figure 6.3).

Ensure an Eye Light

Safe Action Line and Domestic Cutoff

Although technologies are changing rapidly, the traditional 4:3 "tube"-based television set is still popular in the homes of many people. As a receiver and display monitor for picture information, it has done a valiant job, but it suffers from a peculiarity known as **domestic cutoff**. The TV set actually "cuts off" or does not display the outer edges of the original video or filmed image at the top, bottom, left, and right sides of the screen. This area of lost picture information is roughly 10% in from the edge of the source material. Since camera operators know that this cutoff will eventually happen, they frame their shots within what is called the **safe action zone**.

Many cameras, but not all, will have a line or corner marking on the viewfinder that shows where this safe action area exists 10% in from the real edge of the full image frame. When creating your strong compositions for your shots, you must keep in mind that no real important information or action should ever take place in this outer edge of the frame. You even have to compensate for the appropriate headroom and look room for the final framing that will be visible on the television set or display screen. If you record the image of signs or other written materials, make sure to place them fully visible within the frame away from the edges. There are often markings on the viewfinder known as the **safe title** area for just such a purpose. It is a good practice to keep all important action and composed visual elements well within the safe action zone, especially if you may be shooting 16:9 imagery that might be displayed on the 4:3 screen as well (Figure 6.4).

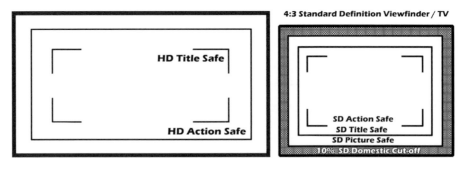

FIGURE 6.4   The safe action line helps keep important visual information away from the edges of the frame in both 4:3 and 16:9 images.

Follow Action with Loose Pan and Tilt Tripod Head

Much of what you record with your shots will involve objects or talent in motion. Whether you are framing a medium shot or a medium close-up, you could run the risk of having the action on screen bump the edges of frame or even break out beyond the boundaries of your frame—usually left, right, or top. It is best to keep all major action away from the edges of your frame, but there will be times where action covers more ground on set or location and you will need to follow the movements of your talent.

Most tripod heads (where you mount the camera) are equipped with pan and tilt capabilities and therefore pan and tilt locks to help keep them stable. When the camera operator is asked to follow action and reframe "on the fly," it is best to have a better quality tripod head and camera support. The more professional equipment allows for smoother and more stable panning and tilting action. The goal of the camera operator is to maintain good framing; if the talent is moving, such as someone pacing the floor, playing tennis, or dancing, it is wise to keep the pan and tilt locks loose. This allows for smooth, minor adjustments of the camera angle as the action unfolds in front of it during the take. This reframing happens all the time, but it is done so smoothly and unobtrusively that it is most often not noticed by the audience. You should aim to do the same (Figure 6.5).

FIGURE 6.5   A camera operator must be ready to reframe during the recording of action.

Shooting Overlapping Action for the Edit

Remember, it is your job as the camera operator to provide the appropriate shots to the editor so that the visual elements will make sense and cut smoothly in the final product. When you have to shoot an action from two or more different angles and you do not have the luxury of operating more than one camera, you will have to have the talent repeat the same action over and over again for each take at each camera position. Overlapping action is the action performed by the talent that is visible from each different camera angle covering the shots for a scene. You need to record this overlapping action in each shot so that the editor will have good and varied choices for creating an "action edit" or a "continuity edit."

Wide shots and medium shots may call for more overlapping action coverage due to their inclusion of more visual elements. Closer shots will not normally require as much overlapping coverage because they tend to highlight details that are magnified on the screen and not as much movement can be recorded for matching from one shot to the next.

Continuity of Action

The camera person cannot make an actor perform identical movements, speak the same lines, or emote in the same way from shot to shot, but she or he can monitor the performances and help gauge whether they will provide the continuity required during the editing process.

Matching Speed of Action

If coverage calls for two medium shots to show a person walking up to a door, turning the doorknob, opening the door, and walking through into the next room, then the action's performance by the talent should be of similar speeds as well as similar movements from one camera angle to the next. However, if you determine that covering a close-up shot of the hand turning the doorknob is an important detail to show the audience, then there will have to be a modification to the speed of execution on the part of the actor. Closer shots of overlapping action should have the movements performed at a slightly slower speed.

A hand traveling into a close-up shot of a doorknob will appear to move much faster across the screen because the screen is only showing the magnified detail of the doorknob and then the "large" hand doing its movement. The less screen space an object or action occupies within the frame, the slower the movement will appear. So, for proper continuity, you may wish to shoot the close-up insert shots with a slightly slower movement of talent, but perhaps shoot just one at normal speed so that the editor will have both choices (Figure 6.6).

Overlapping Too Much Action

There is a danger in shooting too much overlapping action on each camera setup. For the economy of time, money, and energy in both production and postproduction, it is wise to be judicious with your choices of how much or how little overlapping action will need to be captured from each unique camera angle. Too little will provide the editor with inadequate options for cutting the continuity edit, whereas too much may allow a greater choice but will come at the added expense of more time and money being spent on getting the extraneous coverage that may never be used during the edit.

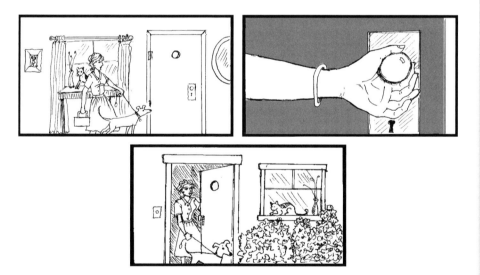

FIGURE 6.6 Talent movements in CU and BCU shots should be performed slightly slower so, when magnified across the entire screen, they appear normal.

Shooting Overlapping Action for the Edit

Shooting Ratio

It should be clear that not every frame shot during production makes it into the final edit of the project. Bad takes, beginnings and endings of shots, coverage not required, and overlapping actions not utilized by the editor will end up on the "cutting room floor" (an expression from film editing days when the unwanted outtakes of the physical strips of emulsion film were thrown on the floor of the edit room). The **shooting ratio** is the relationship between the amount of footage (film or videotape) recorded during production and the amount of footage that makes it into the final edited piece for viewing by an audience. The overall shooting ratio is represented by two numbers separated by a colon (:). As an example, if you used one good take in the final edit, but shot seven different versions of that take, then your shooting ratio for that shot would be 7:1.

Scripted fictional narratives will often have a lower shooting ratio because each shot should be well planned ahead of time. Documentaries may have a larger shooting ratio due to the lack of scripting to action and interviews. Wildlife, travel, and reality television shows can have a huge shooting ratio. It is not always easily predictable what the shooting ratio of a project will become, but it is a good idea to at least generate a best guess ratio when planning your shoot. Budgets are not always about money. Time is a very important factor during production, so the fewer takes you have to roll on the more time is saved all around. A low shooting ratio with a good variety of shot coverage can be a winning combination for everyone (Figure 6.7).

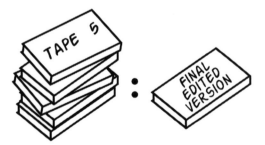

FIGURE 6.7   Five tapes of material edited down to one tape of that material is an example of a 5:1 shooting ratio.

Storyboards and Shot Lists

Whether you are shooting a feature film, a music video, or a 30-second commercial, you would benefit from creating storyboards, overheads, and shot lists before the first day of production begins. **Storyboards** are small drawings that map out what the framing and composition will be for each shot you need to record. The pictures act as templates for the eventual real setups you make, like a comic book version of the motion picture. Storyboards also allow you to see how the various shots necessary to cover the action will edit together once you enter the postproduction phase. The drawings help get everybody involved in the creation of the actual images on the same "visual page."

Overheads can be simple "bird's-eye view" diagrams that map out where on the set you will place camera, talent, lighting fixtures, etc. They help get the crew ready to place the right things in the right places when you get to location or arrive on set. Finally, **shot lists** are a way to account for all of the various shots that you will need to accomplish to get the coverage for a scene. The list is often labeled per scene number with separate letters representing each unique camera angle on action, i.e., scene 1/ shot A/take 1. Creating storyboards and shot lists will be accomplished before the physical shooting actually begins, during a period referred to as **preproduction** (Figure 6.8).

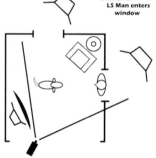

Shot 5: INT -
LS Man enters
window

SHOT LIST - SCENE FIVE

1 - WS Ext House
2 - LS Burglar approach
3 - CU Burglar face be
4 - MS Burglar looks i
5 - LS Dog watches bur

FIGURE 6.8   An example of a storyboard, an overhead schematic, and a partial shot list.

Always Have Something in Focus

It is extremely important that you always have something within your frame in focus. The human visual system, when working correctly, always allows you to see some plane of space around you in proper focus. You have the luxury of automatic focus shifting—meaning that you can be focusing on something 2 inches away from your eye one moment and then focusing on an object very far way the next moment. Camera lenses either have no autofocus capability (film emulsion cameras) or have auto controls that guess at what object you would like to have in focus (video cameras). Controlling your focus manually is usually preferred. You get greater creative control that way.

The main lesson about focus is to have something important to the shot in focus at all times. Humans do not see "out of focus" by design (unless you require prescription corrective lenses and do not wear them). We do not like to watch blurry images because it is unnatural and we reject it. That is why compromised framing or less than solid composition might be overlooked by a viewer, but any out-of-focus (blurry or soft focus) shot stands out like a sore thumb. There are special cases and allowances for creative uses of blur if the shot is a subjective POV and the camera represents the altered perceptions of an inebriated or semiconscious character. Music videos often experiment with radical focus shifting as well.

FIGURE 6.9 A series of shots illustrating a lack of focus shift and then a rack focus from the woman to the background.

As an example, let us say that your frame has one female character in a close-up shot. If the depth of field of the shot is shallow enough, only the woman is in focus and the background is blurry. Creatively, this helps keep the attention of the audience on the woman and not on other objects behind her in the frame. However, if the woman fully exits frame and the focal plane does not alter, then the background will remain blurry and the audience is left watching an empty blurry frame until the next shot cuts on to the screen. It is almost always best to **rack focus** to the background **focal plane** as soon as the character fully exits the frame. This way the audience is watching the woman (in focus) leave the frame and then their eyes can immediately rest on the background, which has come into sharp focus. There is no awkward feeling or moment of confusion on the part of the viewer. This is critical especially just before a cut to a new shot or new scene. The quick, smooth transition in the plane of focus to the background gives something in focus for the viewer's eye to watch as the shot ends (Figure 6.9).

Always Have Something in Focus

Frame for Correct "Look Room" on Shots That Will Edit Together

Let us say you are recording a medium shot of two people facing each other having a simple conversation. You will most likely also get coverage of tighter, clean singles, more commonly called close-ups. When you compose for the CU of the person on the left, you will most likely place their head along the 1/3 "line" on frame left, allowing them to look across the empty space over to frame right. The shot of the other character will be mirrored in its composition, with the head on frame right looking across the void to frame left. This composition mimics what the wider two-shot had already established regarding the empty space in between the two characters. The eye-lines of the talent trace back and forth across the empty space in between and, as a result, the audience will do the same when the two CU shots are edited together.

This same technique can be used between a person and any object at which they may look. In one shot, a person frame left may be looking off frame right at some object. When you record the shot of that object, it should be placed over on frame right in order to allow the appropriate space between (the look room) even though the inanimate object does not look back at the person. When these two shots are cut together, the eye-line traces across to screen right on shot one and continues that direction in shot two until the viewer's eye rests upon the object of interest. It would be rather awkward to frame people or objects such that when they are cut together they appear to butt up against one another as in Figure 6.10.

FIGURE 6.10   It is important to follow lines of attention and allow for proper look room space when composing closer shots of people and objects that will be cut together.

Frame for Correct "Look Room" on Shots That Will Edit Together

Shoot Matching Camera Angles When Covering Dialogue

With a traditional approach to shooting a simple dialogue scene you would most likely begin by covering the wide or establishing shot, moving the camera for a tighter two-shot, and then finally moving in for over-the-shoulders and clean single CUs. Working this way, you allow for the broadest moves first, and the talent gets to match their lines and action better. The lighting also gets easier as you move in for closer shots because you do not need to pay as much attention to the entire set, but just on the talent's face. The important lesson for the camera operator to remember is that although the close-up shots may be shot last, they should be thought about ahead of time to check for how they will be physically shot in that environment. Will there be room for the camera to move to get the shots? Will there be any problems with background objects? Will lighting or depth of field pose any issues?

The reason all of this matters so much is that you should always be aiming for matching shots when you shoot coverage of the scene beyond the master wide shot. This is not referencing matching actor continuity because that should always be attended to, but we are talking about matching the framing and composition of your tighter coverage shots within a scene. Your goal should be to use the same camera distance, same lens focal length, same depth of field, and the same or very similar lighting. The framing and composition of the single close-up shots should mirror one another.

As usual, how things eventually edit together helps dictate how they should be originally recorded. When you cover the two individuals talking in this simple scene, their close-up shots and over-the-shoulder shots should match or mirror one another. This way, when the editor gets to cut the scene together, the viewer sees the wide shot and understands the overall scene's lighting and character placement in the film space. Then, when CU shots are cut back to back, the audience is given matching "mirrored" shots and knows how to place these individuals within the larger film space outside the CU frame. Mismatched shots cut in a back-and-forth fashion will confuse and possibly annoy the viewer because the information being presented is not harmonious.

This process and the ultimate edited presentation of these shots in the motion picture are generally called **shot-reverse-shot**. The coverage shots for one character are shot all the way through into the closest framing and then camera and lighting can switch over to cover the shots for the remaining character. In our example, the first MCU is shot from +45 degrees around the 180 degree arc and, eventually, the other character is covered in an MCU from −45 degrees (see Figure 6.11). You get matching imagery for the edit, and the shot-reverse-shot is completed.

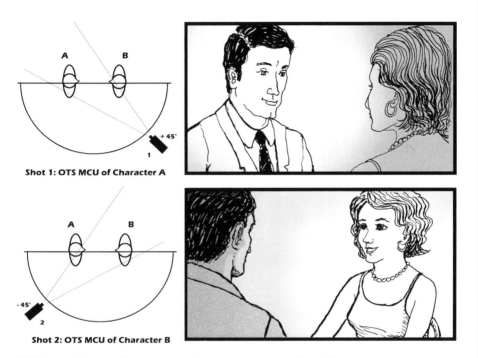

Shot 1: OTS MCU of Character A

Shot 2: OTS MCU of Character B

FIGURE 6.11   Shoot matching shot-reverse-shot coverage for proper editing choices.

Shoot Matching Camera Angles When Covering Dialogue

Place Important Objects in the Top Half of Your Frame

The eyes of a motion picture audience member will normally gravitate to the top half of the picture frame. We normally view things from the top down (pages of a book, a person walking at us, etc.). Compositionally speaking, the space about one-third down from the top will be a zone occupied by the eyes of human characters when shot in close-up so this phenomenon makes sense. Filmmakers have taken advantage of this and created meaning around an object's placement within the frame. Objects (including people's heads) that are placed in the top half of the frame receive more attention from the viewer—the objects have more "weight" or visual presence and are assigned a greater importance within the scene or story. Objects placed lower in the frame tend to have less "weight," have less visual presence, and are less important in the story.

This does not mean that you should never put important objects in the lower half of your frame. The important thing is to think about object importance and about how the viewing audience will look at your frame on screen and how they will digest the visual information that you present to them. Many interesting compositions utilize the entire frame and often allow or compel the viewer's eyes to roam around the frame looking for the bits that interest them or that may have a deeper meaning to the overall motion picture. Lighting can certainly help with this eye direction, but the top half/bottom half guideline does come into play quite often, however. An example is a wider two-shot where a more powerful character stands over the seated figure of the less powerful character. An up/down power dynamic is created (Figure 6.12).

FIGURE 6.12 Objects placed higher in the frame hold more visual "weight" or importance. A viewer's eye is trained to look there first.

Be Aware of the Color Choices Made Throughout Your Project

Although they do not have to be, color choices can be very important to a motion picture. A particular color can take on a particular meaning—red could mean a warning or denote passion, whereas blue could mean a cold or uncaring individual or a sterile environment. Even if you do not take your color scheme that far into implied meaning, the color choices that are made for set dressing, costumes, and make-up will have an impact on how the shots get recorded and how visible certain objects might be. For instance, you may not wish to put a character clothed in all dark clothing in front of a shadowy or dark-colored wall for the fear that he will get "lost" in the sea of darkness.

There is a science to color and light and you should certainly explore more of that on your own. Just be aware that bright colors will tend to appear closer to a viewer (as though they were popping off the screen), whereas darker colors appear to be farther away like they were receding into the background. This phenomenon could help you create particular areas of visual attention by juxtaposing bright and dark color areas within your sets and wardrobe. Beyond the colors of paint and fabrics, you can also apply colored **gels** to light fixtures in order to create color washes across people and environments—most commonly seen as blue for cool moonlight at night and orange for warm interior night lights. There are also color altering processes that you can do during the postproduction phase of a project that work on either emulsion film or digital video being edited on a computer (Figure 6.13).

FIGURE 6.13   The colors or tones of wardrobe and set dressing can play a major role in your image creation. Beware of combining dark clothes with dark backgrounds.

Always Be Aware of Headroom

An important part of your compositional considerations should always be headroom—how much or how little space you allow at the top of the frame for a person's hair or hat, etc. Too much headroom will force the eyes and face of a character too low in the frame. Too little headroom will raise them too high in the frame or simply look wrong due to the chopping off of the forehead and so forth. If you have to err in one direction, however, you should have less headroom. Why? Well, when you give too much and force the face lower in the frame, you also force the mouth and chin lower. As the person speaks it is very likely that the bottom of the chin and jaw will break below the bottom edge of the frame in a CU shot. Since the top of the human head does not traditionally move, it is safer to lose that above the top edge of frame, thus keeping the chin and jaw fully visible in the frame as the person speaks (Figure 6.14).

Consistent headroom across shots in a shot-reverse-shot scenario is also important, as is the headroom of a documentary interviewee. In the latter case, while shooting a subject for a long question-and-answer period for a documentary, it is important that the camera operator maintain correct headroom throughout the shoot. The editing may call for shots to be placed in any order and if there is largely differing headroom among the shots it may look awkward when cut near one another in the final piece. As a final important tidbit about shooting "talking heads" for a documentary, try not to reframe drastically while the subject is speaking. Very slight pans and tilts may be necessary to keep proper framing as the subject moves around in his/her seat, but you should not try to drastically alter your zooming focal length or alter focus while the subject is giving the answer to a question. If you do, it will most likely make that portion of the visuals unusable for the editor. You should wait until the subject stops speaking and then reframe and adjust focal length and focus.

FIGURE 6.14   Always aim for proper headroom in your shots.

Keep Distracting Objects Out of the Shot

Many of you have seen a live news report on location when a passerby waves vigorously at the camera from behind the standing reporter. The out-of-place movements distract our attention away from the main point of the report and the impact is lost. A small crew on a live news report cannot do much to prevent these distractions, but any nonlive shoot should allow for some control over the set. As a camera operator, it would be your job to verify that the frame was clean and that no objects, either moving or stationary, would prove to be a visual distraction for a viewing audience.

The main goal is to keep the composition strong. Any object that has noticeable movements or bright colors or an odd shape can compromise the good composition by acting as an eye magnet to the viewer. If you shoot a CU of a person's head, make sure that no strange lines, shapes, or objects come "out" from behind their head. This can have a comical effect when done intentionally, but for the most part, frame these shots so that no distracting objects either obscure the face in the foreground or "grow" out of the head from the background. The same can be said for any "talking head" interview CU shot for a documentary. Active TV sets, computer monitors, and even windows to the outside world can draw the viewer's eye away from the main subject. Either do not incorporate these items in the shot or blur them out through creating a very shallow depth of field (Figure 6.15).

FIGURE 6.15 Try to keep your frame clean and free of distracting objects, especially near the heads of talent.

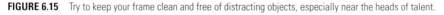

Use the Depth of Your Film Space to Stage Shots with Several People

Simple shots of one or two persons allow ample screen space to compose their blocking and placement within a simple frame. When your shot must contain a larger number of people (even with the modern wide screen aspect ratio of HD video) you will have to find creative ways to layer the multiple subjects deeper into the third dimension of the film space. The foreground, middle ground, and near background become a combined zone where persons can be blocked or staged to fit within the frame. As seen through the camera's lens, the bodies of the people will have a slight overlap, but the faces should all be clearly visible and discernible.

The actual blocking will depend on the physical space of the set or location, the set dressing or furnishings within the space, and the size of the individuals. For groups of six to ten people you may need to have some sitting and some standing and all at different distances from the camera's lens. If the group is larger or needs to be a crowd, there will eventually be a point where an overlap of faces will occur and most will not be discernible. In that event, place the most knowable or important people nearer to camera so the audience can still see their faces and recognize them for who they are. It is not often desirable to have one or more characters whose head is turned away from camera, but you might find that to have all heads facing the same direction looks awkward, unnatural, or too subjective. When the variables are finally known to you on the day of shooting, you should quickly experiment with the best blocking options that take advantage of the depth of the film space (Figure 6.16).

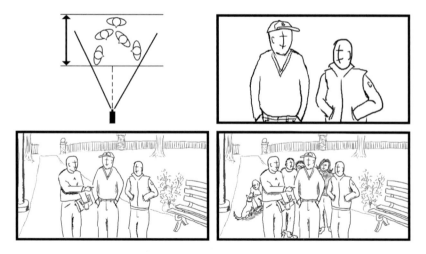

FIGURE 6.16   Use the depth of the film space to help stage the bodies when more people must occupy the frame.

In a Three Person Dialogue Scene, Matching Two Shots Can Be Problematic for the Editor

By staging three people standing across the width of the frame in a wide shot, you establish the position and spatial relations among the people. For this example, let us label the person on screen left as character A, the person in the middle as B, and the person frame right as C. You would normally continue to get coverage of the scene by moving in for the two-shot. In this case, you could get a two-shot of A and B and you could get a two-shot of B and C. The issue arises during the edit session.

In two-shot #1, character A will be frame left and B will be on frame right, but in two-shot #2, character B will be frame left and C will be frame right. If you cut #1 next to #2, you will clearly see character B jump from frame right to frame left. This will prove rather distracting and be unacceptable to a viewing audience. Although you should shoot both two-shots mentioned earlier, you also need to shoot single close-up shots of all three characters so that the editor will have the best possible shot options when the cutting process begins (Figure 6.17).

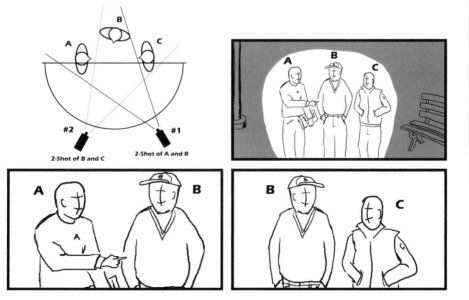

FIGURE 6.17   Two-shots in a three person dialogue scene will not cut together well. Give the editor better options by also shooting clean singles of all three characters.

Try to Always Show Both Eyes of Your Subject

Since the eyes of your subject act as a magnet for the eyes of the viewer and much of the emotional or mental state of the character is conveyed via the eyes in a close-up or a big close-up shot, you would be well served to make sure the eyes are readily visible. We have already discussed the use of the **eye light** to bring attention to the eyes, but we should mention that a **3/4 profile** shot is also a highly desirable blocking/camera angle to cover the individual in the closer shots.

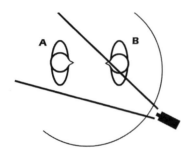

Character A Over-The-Shoulder 3/4 Profile

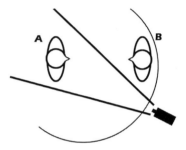

Character A 3/4 Profile MCU

FIGURE 6.18 Find the appropriate angle for your shot, but remember to favor your talent's eyes as much as possible. The diagrams illustrate how to turn an OTS into a clean single shot.

The 3/4 profile allows the camera lens to see and record both eyes of the subject. This same angle on the subject would work for an over-the-shoulder shot as well, but you may have to play with the physical distance between the actors in order to get the framing correct. If you wanted to quickly change an over-the-shoulder shot into a clean single close-up in 3/4 profile, you would have to ask the actor whose back is to camera to step back a few paces in order to clear the frame. Keeping that now out-of-frame actor nearby will maintain the eye-line of the actor being recorded in the CU (see diagrams in Figure 6.18).

Remember that a straight to camera shot will reveal both eyes, yes, but when the talent looks directly into lens the shot becomes entirely a subjective shot, which is less appropriate for drama and more appropriate for news casting. A full profile shot is also a specialty shot, as only one side of the talent's face is visible and the one eye that is visible cannot really be "looked into" as it stares straight forward (directly frame left or frame right). Of course, you should use any talent position or camera angle that you feel is appropriate and conveys your meaning or makes visible your intended information. The 3/4 profile is just a very solid approach to shooting closer shots and it will not disappoint the audience.

Try to Always Show Both Eyes of Your Subject

Be Aware of Eye-Line Directions in Closer Shots

Eye-line traces across film space to unite the subject's gaze to some object of interest. Whether the object of interest is another person, a picture frame, a car outside of a window, or a menacing cloud in the sky does not matter. What does matter is the direction in which the actor's eyes look when you cover them in a medium shot or closer. Wider shots convey general directions and head placement will matter, but close shots reveal more detail and place a keener emphasis on eye-line.

Generally, when the camera operator looks at the talent through the camera's viewfinder he or she will have to gauge how accurate the eye-line of the actor is. Does it match the direction of the eye already established in the wider shots? Since close-up shots magnify the features, it may be necessary to modify the actual direction an actor is looking. The important thing is to ensure that the eye-lines for all concerned characters match in their individual shots. The angle or direction of the gaze will often just not look correct and you will have to talk the talent into the right path. It is often helpful if someone behind or around the camera holds a tracking object, such as their closed fist, in order to get the talent to establish the new and correct eye-line for your closer shots (Figure 6.19).

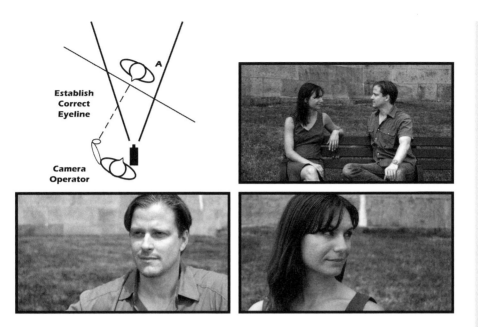

FIGURE 6.19 Talent's eye-line must match from wide shots into closer shots. You may have to talk the talent into establishing a new object of interest on set for a better eye-line. The man's eye-line works well, but the woman's eye-line is too far behind its "mark."

Understand When and How to Perform a Zoom during a Shot

Zoom lenses allow you to record frames at various focal lengths. The **angle of view** runs from wide to narrow. If the camera is locked down, then a "zoom in" simply magnifies the center of the wider frame. The optical shifting that a zoom lens allows is not possible with our human eyes so therefore the resulting motion is alien to our normal visual processing and stands out rather vividly. Many might say that you should never use a zoom action during the recording of a shot, but that is too limiting a view of the creative possibilities that a zoom lens can offer. Just be aware that since zooms change the focal length, they will also alter the depth of field so be conscious of your focus.

Straight up zooms and even "snap zooms" (very fast zooms) have their place in our modern film catalog. One often thinks of films from the 1970s or even "kung-fu" movies, but just because you have the ability to perform a zoom does not mean that you have to. You may find that a focal length change during a shot is very desirable. It may be a rather effective practice to "hide" your zoom in or zoom out by combining the focal

Shot 1 Part A:
Neutral Wide Angle
at Ground Level

Shot 1 Part B:
Tilt Up and Zoom In
at Same Time

FIGURE 6.20   Hiding a lens zoom within a pan or tilt is often very effective. Framing and focal length changes are made at the same time to alter composition and perspective.

length change with a panning or tilting action. The camera's reframing helps cover the more unnatural action of the zoom. Of course, it also depends on what type of project you are shooting, for the viewing public has grown quite accustomed to zooming shots when presented in news stories or photojournalist documentaries where the camera must remain further away from the action for safety reasons. Very, very slow zooms can also be incorporated into a very long take where the focal length change is so subtle over time that it is not really noticed by the engrossed audience member (Figure 6.20).

Understand When and How to Perform a Zoom during a Shot

Motivate Your Truck In and Truck Out Dolly Moves

All shots, whether static or moving, should be motivated, but this holds additionally true for dolly shots that either push into a set or pull out of it. Usually the motion of an object or a character is ample motivation to truck in. The camera will seek out more detail and more information as it explores a deeper area of the set or an enlarged section of the visible area of interest. This pushing in and exploring is a natural move and replicates what a human might do in order to see more detail—get closer to the item of concern.

Trucking out, however, is a more unnatural movement. The reverse motion of the truck out implies a person leaving a scene walking backward—not something that humans are likely to do on a regular basis. If a character or object is moving toward the camera and the camera wishes to truck out in order to keep the character or object in frame, then that provides the motivation for the unnatural move. Because a truck out usually reveals larger areas of the environment, they can show more visual consequences of the story or of a character's action. Therefore, one is most likely to find a truck out at the end of a scene or at the end of an entire motion picture. The truck out provides a visual overview of some event or action and, when coupled with a crane boom or a helicopter mount, acts as a final summation to the story, leaving the characters to continue their lives without the further observation of the camera—or the viewing audience (Figure 6.21).

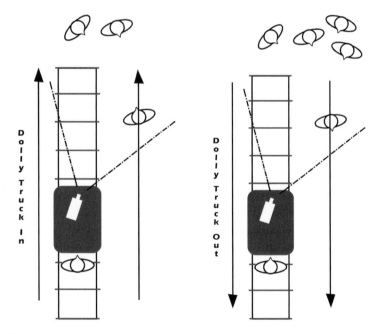

FIGURE 6.21 Talent movement can motivate truck in and truck out dolly moves.

Ways to Cross the 180 Degree Line Safely

We know that when covering shots for a scene, the camera should normally stay on only one side of the set within the 180 degree circular arc. We do this so that when the various shots of that scene's coverage are edited together, the screen direction of movements and the eye-lines of characters match the established spatial relations found in the wider master shot. There may be times when you wish to move the camera around the set and get new angles on action from the opposite or "incorrect" side of the axis of action. This can be done but there are some special ways to do it without it being jarring to the viewing audience.

If you provide motivation such as the movement of talent or the action of an object, then you can cross the camera over the action line during the continuous shot in order to provide continuous coverage of the movement or action in the same film space. The original 180 degree line is established with the first shot, but the line is then changed and updated as the camera moves to follow the motivation (talent with new sight lines) around the set.

If you establish the line in the first shot and then move the camera to the farthest extreme along the arc without going over the line, you will have created a neutral shot for use during the edit process. Since that 180 degree extreme location for the camera "sits on the fence," you would be then free to fall to the other side of the line and shoot from the new side. The new line being established after the neutral shot in between allows the audience to reset their spatial understanding of the film space.

You may also try to use a **cutaway** shot to a related object or person within the same film space. If you provide shots from both sides of the action line, but you have also recorded cutaways or insert shots for the editor, then the cutaway can break the spatial attention of the viewer and the next shot may be shown from the far side of the original axis of action. The majority of the film space and the blocking of the characters should be established in the wider shots already in order to allow the audience to jump from one shot to the cutaway to the new line shot (Figure 6.22).

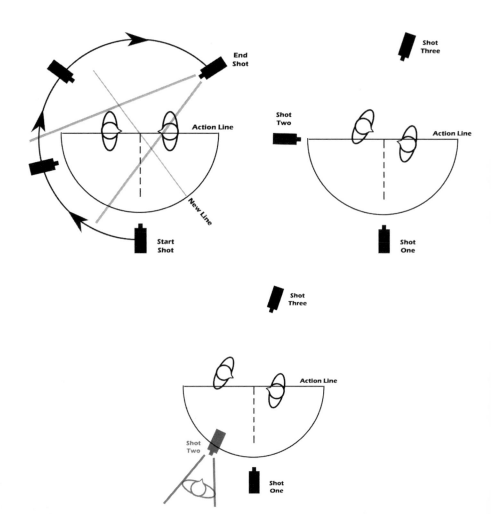

FIGURE 6.22 Three ways to move the camera across the 180 degree line safely.

Allow the Camera More Time to Record Each Shot

We all know that time and money are very important to all motion picture projects no matter what the medium, format, story, or type of event being shot. Usually, however, the ultimate goal is to pass on all production footage to the edit team and have them piece together the final presentation. It is very important then that you provide the post-production crew with as much usable footage as possible, which means making sure that each take of each shot has plenty of start-up time and plenty of completion time.

It is wise to get the camera "**rolling**" before any critical action happens. This allows all equipment the time required to get up to operating "**speed**" and it gives the talent and crew time to settle. Rolling camera before "Action!" is called also provides the editor with critical extra footage at the **head** of the shot. She or he can then potentially use this extra footage to pad out the timing of the shots during the edit.

A similar process should be followed at the end of the shot. As the documentary event ends or the director calls "Cut!" the camera operator should allow a few more seconds of recording time. This ensures that all critical action was captured by the camera and also provides that critical extra footage at the **tail** of the shot for the editor to play with. Since it is your job, as camera operator, to provide the most usable footage to the editor, this practice of rolling early and cutting late will help you win a friend for life (Figure 6.23).

Allow the Camera More Time to Record Each Shot

HOW TO "CALL THE ROLL"

1. "LOCK IT UP!"
2. "EVERYONE SETTLE. THIS IS FOR A TAKE."
3. "ROLL SOUND" – IF RECORDING SEPARATELY
4. "ROLL CAMERA"
5. VOICE / PICTURE SLATE (SCENE + TAKE)
6. "MARK IT"
7. CLOSE THE SLATE'S CLAP STICKS – 'CLACK!'
8. PAUSE A MOMENT OR TWO
9. "ACTION!"
10. ACTION BEGINS
11. ACTION ENDS
12. PAUSE A MOMENT OR TWO
13. "CUT!"

FIGURE 6.23 Rolling the camera early and stopping it late will ensure the extra "padding" footage often needed during the edit. Slating shots will help identify them during postproduction.

Allow All Actions to Complete before Cutting Camera

There may be many occasions where this practice is neither possible nor prudent, but, for the most part, it should be followed for it makes a great deal of sense. It is the job of the editor to decide when to cut into a shot and when to cut out of a shot. The camera operator should cover all of the action so that the editor has that footage from which to make his or her best choice for the cut.

If an actor is to walk out of frame, let them walk fully out of frame and allow the empty space to be recorded for a short while. The same goes for a car, plane, dog, and so forth. Allow the exit action to complete and let the camera run for a bit longer. These extra frames can be of particular importance if the editor decides to create a dissolve or fade or some other transition that will imply the passage of time before the next shot, most likely in a different location or time period, is cut in. If the action calls for something to fall, a door to close, or a person to round the corner of a building and disappear from view, then let all those actions complete in the shot before you cut camera. The static end frame of a pan or tilt will also provide the opportunity for the recorded action to be completed at the end of the camera move (Figure 6.24).

FIGURE 6.24   Allow actions to complete before stopping the camera.

During Documentary Shooting Be as Discrete as Possible

When you are on location shooting documentary footage it can become very challenging to acquire the shots that you need without raising a lot of attention for yourself and your crew. You will most likely attain the best results by remaining discrete, being respectful, and working quickly. As a crew member working on any project it would be wise to remain discrete, respectful, and efficient but these working practices might get you more mileage when working in foreign or potentially hostile environments.

You should, first of all, obtain all required permissions and certificates so that you can shoot at these locations legally. Your goal is to observe and record, not intrude or stage the events. The more people who are aware of who you are and what your purpose is, the more likely you are to get negative attention or simply have people behave differently than they normally might. The advancements in equipment—small digital video and audio recorders—will help you keep your "footprint" smaller, allowing for more discrete operations. Film emulsion cameras still tend to be a bit bulkier and their rarity causes more curiosity in onlookers. Remember to obey all local laws and respect the privacy of individuals who do not wish to be a part of your project.

During Documentary Shooting Be as Discrete as Possible

Beware of Continuity Traps While Shooting a Scene

While you shoot coverage for a scene in a motion picture you are certainly paying attention to matching dialogue delivery, action or motion, camera angles, eye-line, and so forth. There may be many things, however, beyond the basics that can cause a continuity headache. The important thing is to be observant and thorough. Continuity issues can make the postproduction process difficult, so try to avoid them during production.

Continuity traps tend to be objects on set or around the shooting location that will change over time. Since shooting all of the coverage for a particular scene or event can take a long time, these continuity traps will appear differently from one shot to another when the coverage is edited together during postproduction. These secondary continuity errors may not be as noticeable as actor movement or eye-line matching but they are still potential sources of audience annoyance.

Be aware of functional clocks or large watches that will reveal the passage of time when shooting chronologically but will cause a continuity issue when the scene is edited. The same goes for the movement of the sun. Either bright sunshine or the resulting shadow movement will jump around from shot to shot during the edited piece. You may not have any control over the sunlight, but you could structure your shooting schedule around it or change the framing so that it does not become an issue. Any background activity, such as an active TV set, people, and cars, should be either removed or made to do the same thing in each medium or close-up shot you need to take that may involve their participation. Finally, audio concerns should be addressed, such as airplanes, automotive vehicle sounds, telephones ringing, and especially uncontrollable music. All of these could potentially pose a threat to smooth editing (Figure 6.25).

FIGURE 6.25 Be aware of continuity traps like these.

Use Short Focal Length Lenses to Hide Camera Movement

The **field of view** or angle of view that a lens provides depends on its focal length. A wide lens—a lens that is set to a short focal length such as 10 mm—captures a larger field of view and therefore creates an image that shows more of the environment in front of the camera. When you see more of the environment, objects tend to appear smaller. If the camera were to move or shake while recording a shot, as with a hand-held camera, the smaller objects in the frame do not travel about very much because of the relative distances they have to traverse in the wider image. The larger distances between objects and their relationship to the horizon line will help them appear more stable if the camera experiences a minor shake or wobble.

Conversely, a long lens set to telephoto—a long focal length such as 100 mm—captures a much narrower field of view. Since the job of this lens setting is to magnify details of a narrow slice of the environment, the objects within the frame are enlarged and will have less distance to travel around the frame before they hit an edge or leave the frame all together. This is why a handheld camera with a long focal length lens is likely to create an extremely shaky and motion blurred image. Magnified objects in a narrow field of view make even small movements appear like large shifts in spatial stability. As a result, try to use short focal lengths when you need help stabilizing hand-held camera coverage (Figure 6.26).

FIGURE 6.26 A wider lens angle provides more stability if the camera shakes.

Beware of Wide Lenses When Shooting Close-Up Shots

You may use any lens you like so long as it suits the shot and can get the job done. You should be aware, however, of what a lens will do for your image in both a positive way and potentially a negative way. We all understand that wide lenses capture a large field of view and that they tend to have a larger depth of field. The curvature of the optics involved can also exaggerate the perspective, warping the final image from the center outward. The shorter the focal length, the more exaggerated the warped perspective. Extreme versions of this optical phenomenon are called "fish-eye" lenses.

If you set your lens to the shortest focal length and reduce the camera to subject distance in order to get a close-up shot, you will most likely encounter this warped perspective exaggeration. The individual's nose will appear larger and perhaps bulbous, almost poking out at the camera, whereas the ears and the remainder of the head will appear to recede from the camera and appear smaller. This treatment is often used for a comic effect or when one wishes to show a "nightmare" state of consciousness. For normal CU work, however, you may be better served to use a longer focal length setting on your lens and move the camera further away from talent. Much like still photographers who use longer lenses to take portraits, you can reduce the exaggerated perspective of the subject by "flattening" the recorded space. The reduced depth of field may also help isolate the facial features and bring more attention to the CU while the background blurs (Figure 6.27).

FIGURE 6.27   Wide lenses in close can distort facial features in a CU. A longer focal length from slightly farther away can help keep the "portrait" perspective normal.

Control Your Depth of Field

You should always be aware of your depth of field—the range of objects seen to be in acceptable focus and extend into the depth of your shot. The DOF can be controlled (greater or smaller) and shifted within the film space (closer or further from camera). Remember that the nature of optics will provide you with only one **critical plane of focus** in front of the camera's lens. Whatever lives exactly at that distance from the camera will be in sharpest focus. The DOF operates around this one critical focus plane and its horizontal depth is segmented into two unequal parts. The first segment (roughly one-third the overall area of good focus) falls before the critical plane, and the second segment (roughly the remaining two-thirds of the good focus depth) falls just behind the critical focus plane.

If you know the several variables that can affect the DOF then you will always know how to control the DOF.

LIGHT—When you use lots of light, either from the sun or from large lighting fixtures, you will need to close down the **iris** of the lens in order to achieve proper exposure. The smaller iris opening (or high f-stop number) allows less light into the camera and causes a larger depth of field, which is why many daylight exterior shots provide you with sharp focus on almost all objects—from very near to the camera out to infinity at the horizon line. When you shoot in very dark spaces, the lens' iris must be opened up very wide, letting in as much light as possible in order to capture a properly exposed image. This wider opening of the lens causes a shallower DOF. You must be cautious when shooting in low light conditions because it is more difficult to keep the important objects within your frame in proper focus.

FOCAL LENGTH—The optics of the camera lens also play a role in how much DOF you get to use. Wide angle lenses, or lenses set to a short focal length such as 10 mm, will offer a greater DOF. Long focal length lenses, set to 75 or 100 mm, will generate a much more shallow DOF.

CAMERA TO SUBJECT DISTANCE—The DOF increases when your subject is far away from camera. The DOF decreases when your subject is very close to the camera.

SIZE AND SENSITIVITY OF THE RECORDING MEDIUM—The sensitivity of your film emulsion or your video camera's CCD and its size and corresponding lenses also play a factor in the depth of field calculation.

It will now be rather simple to imagine a scenario for either a very large DOF or for a very narrow DOF. Placing the camera far away from a subject, with a wide angle lens setting and lots of light will generate a very large DOF. Placing camera rather close to your subject, with a long focal length lens in very dim lighting will generate a rather shallow DOF. Use these guidelines when you wish to keep your subject in focus but blur out your foreground or background objects (Figure 6.28).

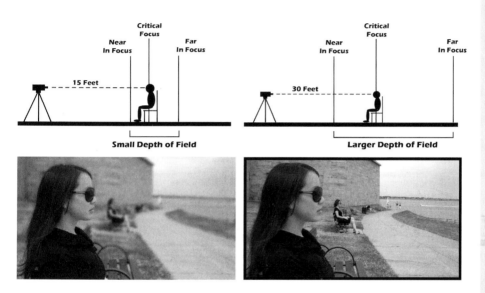

FIGURE 6.28   A shallow depth of field keeps focus on your subject. A larger DOF can incorporate a deeper area within the film space that will also appear to be in sharp focus.

Control Your Depth of Field

Slate the Head of Your Shots

In the film emulsion motion picture world, the images and the sound are recorded by two separate machines. They must be identified and united (also known as synchronized) during postproduction. What helps with this process is the use of a **slate** (see Figure 6.29). These devices used to be made of actual slate way back when and a camera assistant could write important information on them with chalk. Today they are more like a "white board" and you can use dry erase markers to pen down the same types of information. When you record the slate at the beginning of the shot it identifies what the title of the project is, the scene/shot/take being recorded and provides a visual and auditory marker as the wooden slate sticks are "clapped" together.

When shooting video projects, you may have the one camera device capture both picture and sound information. On a digital nonlinear computer-aided edit system, there is no need to "sync" the picture and sound because the digital files from the camera are already married together based on their **time code**. It is still a useful practice to "head slate" the shot on video because it will help identify that shot and make shot organization that much easier for the postproduction team. If you do not have the physical slate to write on and photograph, then you should at least **voice slate** the head of the shot so that everyone will still know what the shot is. There are occasions, especially found

FIGURE 6.29 A slate is used primarily on film sets when two separate devices record picture and sound information. Slates are still useful during the edit process on video shoots where picture and sound are both recorded onto the tape at the same time.

in documentary shooting, where you do not have time to head slate a shot because the reality event begins so abruptly. You can perform what is called a **tail slate**, where you identify the shot after the event has transpired but before you cut the camera's recording. The physical slate is held upside-down for the tail slate. Either way, your main goal is to help identify the shot for easier postproduction workflows.

Slate the Head of Your Shots

End of Chapter Six Review

1. Communicating with talent.
2. Shooting a big close-up or XCU.
3. Ensure an eye light.
4. Camera safe action line and TV domestic cutoff.
5. Follow action with loose pan and tilt tripod head.
6. Shooting overlapping action for the edit.
7. Shooting ratio.
8. Storyboards and shot lists.
9. Always have something in focus.
10. Frame for correct "look room" on shots that will edit together.
11. Shoot matching camera angles when covering dialogue.
12. Place important objects in the top half of your frame.
13. Be aware of the color choices made throughout your project.
14. Always be aware of headroom.
15. Keep distracting objects out of the shot and away from talent's head.
16. Use the depth of your film space to stage shots with several people.
17. In a three person dialogue scene, matching two shots can be problematic for the editor.
18. Try to always show both eyes of your subject.
19. Be aware of eye-line directions in closer shots.
20. Understand when and how to perform a zoom during a shot.
21. Motivate your truck in and truck out dolly moves.
22. Ways to cross the 180 degree line safely.
23. Allow the camera more time to record each shot.
24. Allow all actions to complete before cutting camera.
25. During documentary shooting, be as discrete as possible.
26. Be aware of continuity traps while shooting a scene.
27. Use short focal length lenses to hide camera movement.
28. Be aware of wide lenses when shooting close-up shots.
29. Control your depth of field.
30. Slate the head of your shots.

Chapter Seven
In Conclusion

QUESTION: How is it that so many motion pictures created around the world are understood and appreciated by such a large and diverse viewing audience?

ANSWER: The creators followed the grammar of the shot and spoke in a global visual language that is understood by all who view the final presentation.

This book has presented some of the basic rules of visual grammar in filmmaking, defined a number of different shot types, and offered a few good working practices. None of this material is written in stone and all of it is open to interpretation. Different people may choose to approach things in slightly different ways, which should be viewed as a positive thing. Elaboration, experimentation, and blatant subversion have given rise to many new and interesting approaches to creating and conveying entertainment and information over the years. However, no matter what the technology or what the material to be presented, at the bottom of all the innovation would still lay the basic rules of visual grammar.

Know the Rules Before You Break the Rules

We all know that rules exist to establish fair play, set up safety guidelines, and create commonly accepted working practices. Contrary to popular belief, not all rules were made to be broken. Just as there are rules to tennis, golf, and football, we have discovered in this text that there are rules that govern motion pictures. The grammar of the shot—the film language—has evolved over the last 100 plus years but the basic tenets and guidelines have remained the same. As a result of this standardization of imagery, creators the world over are able to tell stories—or show stories—that are understood by a wide variety of audience members. As with your own written language, you can read the images and comprehend what is going on in the motion picture presentation.

So you can imagine, if the rules of written language were not followed, there would be many people who could not read and comprehend what the words on the page were supposed to mean. The same holds true for the motion picture. Lay out your fictional narrative story, your documentary piece, or your news report by following the established rules of film grammar in such a way that the widest possible audience will understand the imagery and comprehend what you are attempting to convey via the visual elements of the work. When you start with the basics and build upon them you are able to create knowable visual events that, as they grow in complexity, challenge and amaze the viewer. When you break the rules before you know the rules, you will often create a visual experience that might just serve to confuse and alienate the viewer, which is not traditionally the goal of filmmakers.

The Reason for Shooting Is Editing

Unless you are simply shooting coverage of a live event for a telecast, your goal in recording motion images will be to pass along the best possible footage to the editor. You should always remember that you must shoot for the edit. Film production exists so that film postproduction can excel. If you create many beautiful compositions and achieve some very complex moving camera shots, and they are well planned such that they can all be visually integrated in the edit process, then you have done very well. However, if you create excellent individual shots at the expense of the editorial needs then you have done a great disservice to the entire motion picture project. If it does not cut together then either there was no forethought during production or there was no need to shoot it in the first place—the shot has become unusable and no one wants that to be the case.

The film production process, no matter how simple or how elaborate, is never an easy process. The potential for mistakes is always present. Numerous stresses, unplanned events, or last minute changes can always happen. A good solution to alleviating as many of these potential headaches as possible is solid preproduction. Shot lists, storyboards, and, of course, a strong understanding of film language will go a long way in helping you generate visually interesting and informative imagery. Well beyond talent performance, you must also make sure that your shots are technically acceptable for the edit. Have you matched angles, camera distances, and focal lengths on your coverage for a scene? Have you followed action until it completes? Is there good focus on all the right planes within the complex shot? Many aspects of the overall project must be planned and executed correctly for the final product to be as good as it possibly can be, so remember to think about what you are shooting and understand how it will be used during the edit.

Your Shots Should Enhance the Entire Story

The basic shot types discussed in this book will be able to provide you with the basic building blocks for shooting coverage of any motion picture event. If you are shooting for a news report, a sporting event, or a documentary, then you may not have need to move beyond the visual basics to show your audience a worthwhile experience, although increasingly, in the modern era, even these motion image products are getting more advanced visual treatments. It has traditionally been the scripted fictional narrative film that allows for more experimentation in the imagery. Your shot compositions, talent blocking, lens choices, camera angles, and so forth have the potential to support, underscore, and enhance the story being told. They might even, at times, subvert and contradict the apparent story. Either way the images can be used to augment the narrative.

As a quick and easy example, let us say that three people have just found a bag of money. The wide establishing shot shows all three characters (A, B, and C) standing around the open bag with the money visibly spilling out onto a table. The characters, location, and scene are set from this first shot. Then you move in for the coverage. You create a clean single MS on character A, but you only created one medium shot for both B and C to appear on screen together. If there are known tensions between A and the team of B and C, then the cutting between shots of A by himself and B and C grouped together can enhance the narrative by physically showing A as a man alone and B and C together as a unified team "against" the character A.

Involve the Viewer as Much as Possible

Motion pictures really are a participatory experience. It might seem as though most people just sit and watch, but what usually happens when they are viewing good material is that they are actively engaged on many levels. Certainly, they should follow the story, but they will also experience a myriad of emotions and have visceral reactions and responses to the actions on the screen. What you show to the audience, how you choose to show it, and when it gets shown are rather important factors in the success of a motion picture.

One of the main goals of most visual works of storytelling is to keep the viewer engaged. There should always be a need to pay attention. If there is no direct involvement for the majority of a motion picture then it is more likely to be seen as boring by the disinterested viewer. Of course, everyone has different tastes and different stories call for different treatments of picture, sound, and pacing in the edit, but all works should have a way to involve the viewer's senses, brain, and emotions. The visual elements are all within your control when you are the camera operator so at least make a concerted effort to cover all the important information—creativity is not always a requirement, but it can often help broaden the visual impact of a piece.

Remember, on the most basic level, when you show a new shot to the audience they are going to scan it for the important information and, if given time in the editing, they are going to appreciate it for all the aesthetic qualities that were incorporated into its frame: composition, lighting, color, focus, movement, and so on. Because most modern audiences are very well acquainted with the visual grammar of the film language, they can comprehend the important facts presented in the visuals very quickly. From one shot to the next, they are constantly scanning for, observing, and digesting visual information, which generates a sense of expectation within the viewer. If you are failing to provide the viewer with the appropriate information when they expect to see it, then you are either skillfully manipulating their fictional narrative experience or you are deleteriously affecting their documentary experience.

Motivating your shots is extremely important as well. There has to be a reason for the shot to exist. What information does it convey? Can an image "tell" more about the story to the viewing audience than spoken words? When it comes to a fictional narrative (scripted storytelling), "**show, don't tell**" is an excellent rule to follow and it should especially appeal to the more visually minded filmmakers. A wide shot shows a college graduation ceremony in progress. A medium shot shows a young woman

Involve the Viewer as Much as Possible

accepting her college degree on the stage. She looks out to the parents in the audience. A close-up of her father shows that his eyes are tearing up with pride and happiness. The wide shot sets the scene and motivates the exploration of who is getting her degree. The girl's eye-line out to the crowd motivates the CU of the father. His CU reveals new data about his emotional state. Each shot conveys new information, helps progress the narrative, and motivates each successive shot as well.

Try Hard Not to Be Obtrusive

This guideline applies to both how you shoot your coverage and how you behave as a member of a motion picture camera crew. The artifice behind shooting is that in the ideal world your camera should be unnoticed by the viewing audience. It is often said that if an audience member notices a shot then it has become a bad shot. If your hand-held shots are too shaky, your horizon lines are always a bit askew, the focus is off just a bit on the main object of interest, the dolly moves are filled with bumps and jiggles, or your zoom is not smooth, then it is highly likely that your audience will notice these issues and be taken out of the viewing experience. Rather than being engaged, informed, or entertained, they will, instead, be too aware that they are viewing a poorly shot motion picture.

As a member of the camera department crew, it is also very important for you to exhibit a similar level of professional behavior. The camera crew is usually in the thick of the action so what you do can be observed by all those around you. You need to keep your "behind the lens" actions to a minimum during shooting. You could wear dark clothing to help blend in and not be a distraction to the talent performing in front of you. Try not to look directly at talent while they are performing. Always be courteous to all people involved in the project. Keep a cool head and get the shot—once you get it, move on. A good shooting pace keeps your talent and crew fresh and motivated to work hard. Try not to schedule very long shoot days. If you have an exterior shoot planned and the weather turns foul, you should have an alternate interior shoot ready to go as a backup. A professional demeanor, a low profile, and an efficient working style will go a long way in sustaining positive results on the shooting set.

Know Your Equipment

It is imperative that the camera operator knows his/her camera very well. No one else on set is going to be tasked with using it as much. Whether it is a 16 mm emulsion film camera or the latest high definition digital video camera, the camera operator and other members of the camera department crew must know as much as possible about the device and all of the accessories. Experience is a great help here, but if none is had yet for the newer user, then reading the manuals will be a good first step, as would asking questions of other, more knowledgeable users of the equipment. Before the first day of shooting, you should make time to play with the equipment, build the camera rig, take it apart, and handle it so you know how it feels, sounds, and even smells—there is often little use in tasting it.

Preparation goes beyond just being familiar with the equipment. You should be accountable for all of the parts as well. Make sure that you have all the pieces of gear that you need and that they are functional and clean. Charge all batteries the night before your first shoot day and remember to pack them when you leave for the job. Know your lenses. Understand their capabilities and make sure they are clean. When you are in a studio or, especially, on location, designate an area strictly for camera department equipment and ask that other personnel stay clear. Keep your camera gear organized and in their cases whenever possible so that you know exactly where to go when you need something. There is very little tolerance on film sets for time and money being lost to easily avoidable errors.

Be Familiar with Your Subject

During preproduction time, as some must wisely be scheduled before the shoot, you should familiarize yourself with the material in the project. Whether it is a documentary being made or a fictional narrative story being told, you should know the subject matter, the persons involved, and, obviously, the days and order of shooting. Read the entire script if you can get your hands on a copy. Understand the tone of the piece—dark, heavy, light, happy, etc. Be as familiar as possible with the locations if possible. Anticipate the needs of the director and the editor while watching for opportunities to make the entire production better. Good preparation of this kind will put you more at ease while shooting and allow you to work more efficiently should something go amiss.

Understand Lighting—Both Natural and Artificial

Anyone involved in creating good visuals for a motion picture project, whether it is something for television, movies, or the Internet, should have a solid understanding of lighting and how to best utilize it for their shooting purposes. One can spend a lifetime mastering the science behind light and color and also the nuances behind manipulating it correctly for use on film sets, but everybody starts somewhere in that learning process so you should not delay in your own training. Composing great shots or pulling off wild dolly moves is certainly a positive thing, but without the appropriate lighting, all of it could be moot.

It is essential that you understand the basics of lighting—hard light, soft light, motivated light, up-lighting, top lighting, practical set lighting, and so forth. You need to understand that there is lighting used just to get exposure (enough to record your image) and there is lighting for creative purposes. You may highlight certain characters or keep others in silhouette. Have overall high key flat lighting or create strong **Chiaroscuro** with low key lighting. You may also wish to use certain colors that have particular meanings for your story. With all this light around your film set, it is very important to check your camera lens for **light flares**—lights that have their beams point into the lens. This errant light falling into your lens can cause flares on the image and you will most often not wish for this to happen.

When sunlight can be used, it can often save a great deal of time and money. However, as we all know, the sun is always "moving." As the Earth rotates on its axis, the sun appears to arc across the sky. This results in an ever-changing play of light and shadow across the world. When you are using natural sunlight as your primary light source, you should be aware that it will be different in just a matter of minutes to a few hours depending on the time of year and your location around the globe. No matter where you are shooting, you should take some time to familiarize yourself with the availability and course that the sun will take across the sky. Part of your responsibility is to plan the best locations and best times of day when the sun can be used to its best advantage. It might be midmorning, noon, or "golden hour." No matter how you cut it, knowing about light and lighting is going to be a critical part of anyone's motion picture training.

Study What Has Already Been Done

A large part of learning how to make good looking motion pictures is knowing that you should really study what has already been done. Conducting research is an easy, informative, and entertaining way to prepare one's self for almost any shoot. You may watch movies, television programming of all kinds (sit-coms, documentaries, dramas, news shows, music videos, reality, etc.), experimental or avant-garde films, and even animations and motion graphics. Your goal is not to replicate precisely what has already been executed, but to find inspiration and common themes or methods that have been explored before you.

Many visually creative people also turn to art history for ideas, inspiration, or examples of particular practices. Paintings, especially, can be a very rich source of compositional studies, color schemes, use of light and shadow, focus, texture, and so on. As everyone working on the motion picture could see a print of a particular painting or review a series of paintings from a particular artist, the works become a very visual way to relate ideas about color palettes or mood or subject matter. Sculpture, architecture, textiles, and so forth become excellent resources and references for the many people involved in creating the numerous elements that go into the making of a motion picture. Because each shot encompasses all of the elements in the final visual presentation, it makes a great deal of sense for camera people to be well versed in these additional disciplines.

In Summation

The key lesson in all of this material about "The Shot" is that recording motion images, whether it is with an emulsion film movie camera or a digital video camera, is not a matter of simply pointing and shooting. Of course, one can take that approach and it may do well for recording birthday parties and holidays, but any professional grade project that is worth doing is worth doing well, which means that you will have to employ a great deal of film language. The basics, as introduced in this book, will have to be understood and incorporated into your projects—at least what applies to your project, for not every shot type, camera move, or lens angle will fit into the visual style that you plan for each project. The idea is to have an ever-expanding tool set and an ever-growing collection of references and resources so that you move from being just an inspired technician to an artful and effective communicator with film language. When you know the grammar of the shots, your shots will tell your story.

Glossary
Grammar of the Shot

180 Degree Line—The imaginary line established by the sight lines of talent within a shot that determines where the 180 degree arc of safe shooting is set up for the camera coverage of that scene. The camera should not be moved to the opposite side of this action line because it will cause a reversal in the established screen direction. See also 180 Degree Rule, Axis of Action, Sight Line.

180 Degree Rule—In filmmaking, an imaginary 180 degree arc, or half circle, is established on one side of the shooting set once the camera first records an angle on the action in that space. All subsequent shots must be made from within that same semicircle. Since screen direction, left and right, for the entire scene is established, the camera may not photograph the subject from the other side of the circle without causing a reversal in the screen direction.

30 Degree Rule—A cousin to the 180 degree rule, this rule decries that when recording coverage for a scene from differing camera angles within the film set, the camera should be moved around the 180 degree arc at least 30 degrees from one shot to the next in order to create enough variation on the angle on action so that the two different shots will edit together and appear different enough in their framing.

4:3—The aspect ratio for standard definition television. Four units wide by three units tall—more square in its visual presentation than the more modern high definition 16:9 video display.

Act (noun)—In long form programming (feature films or episodic television, etc.) the "story" is broken down into several major sections known as acts. In fictional narrative filmmaking, a story will traditionally have three acts—loosely termed the set-up, the confrontation, and the resolution.

Action—What the director calls out to signify that the acting for the shot being recorded should begin.

Angle of Incidence—The angle from which incident light falls upon a film set. A single lighting fixture directly overhead will have a 90 degree (from horizon) angle of incidence.

Angle of View—The field of view encompassed by the light gathering power of a film lens. A wide angle lens has a wide angle of view. A telephoto lens has a more narrow angle of view on the world.

Angle on Action—The angle from which a camera views the action on the film set.

Aperture—In motion picture equipment terms, the aperture refers to the iris or flexible opening of the camera lens that controls how much or how little light is used to expose the image inside the camera. A wide aperture or iris setting lets in a larger amount of light. A smaller aperture lets in less light. On many camera lenses, the aperture can also be fully "stopped down" or closed all the way for total darkness on the image.

Artificial Light—Any light generated by a man-made device such as a film light, a desk lamp, or a neon sign.

Aspect Ratio—The numerical relationship between the dimensions of width and height for any given visual recording medium. In the example 16:9, the first number, 16, represents the units of measure across the width of a high definition video frame. The second number, 9, represents the same units of measure for the height of the same frame.

Atmospherics—Any particulates suspended in the air around a film set or location, such as fog, mist, or dust, which will cumulatively obscure the distant background.

Attention—The direction in which a character faces within the film space. The attention of a character may be drawn by another character, an inanimate object, or anything that attracts his/her gaze. An imaginary line connects the eyes of the character and the object of their attention and, most often, an audience member will trace this line in order to also see what the character sees. See also Sight Lines.

Axis of Action—The invisible line created by talent sight lines that helps establish what side of the action the camera can record coverage for that scene. The camera should not be moved to the opposite side of this action line because it will cause a reversal in the established screen direction. See also 180 Degree Rule, Sight Line, Imaginary Line.

Back Light—A light used on a film set placed behind the talent but pointed at their backside. It generally serves to help separate the body from the background by providing a rim or halo of light around the edges of the body, head/hair.

Background—The zone within a filmed frame that shows the deep space farther away from camera. Most often the background is out of focus, but serves to generate the ambience of the location.

Binocular Vision (Human Visual System)—Having two eyes located at the front of the head. The slight distance between the two eyes causes the human to see nearby objects from two distinct vantage points. The brain then combines the two distinct images into one picture where the overlapping elements take on a three-dimensional aspect.

Blocking—The movement of talent within the film space and the corresponding movement, if any, of the camera in order to follow the actions of the moving talent.

Boom Arm—Deriving its name from the armature on a sailing ship's mast, a boom arm is used to swivel and extend the camera's placement in order to get sweeping shots or keep the camera buoyant without a tripod directly beneath it.

Break Frame—When an object being recorded accidentally moves to the edge of the frame and falls outside the visible area of the image.

Camera Angle—The angle at which a camera views a particular scene. Camera angles can be based on horizontal camera positioning around the subject or vertical camera positioning below or above the subject.

Camera Person/Camera Operator The person, man or woman, who physically handles the camera during the shooting, whose main responsibility is to maintain proper framing and composition and to verify good focus.

Camera Setup—A place on the film set where a camera is positioned to record a shot. Each time the camera is physically moved to a new position it is considered a new camera setup.

Camera Support (Tripods, Etc.)—Any device or piece of film equipment that is used to support the motion picture camera. Tripods, dollies, and car mounts are all examples of various kinds of camera support.

Canted Angle—See Dutch Angle.

Charge-Coupled Device (CCD)—The electronic light sensor built into most video cameras whose job is to turn light wave energy into electronic voltages, which get recorded as brightness and color values on a tape or hard drive in the camera.

Chiaroscuro—Italian for light/dark, the term is used in the visual arts to talk about the high contrast ratio between light areas of a frame and dark areas. Filmmakers, as well as painters, use this technique to show or hide certain visual elements within their frames.

Clean Single—A medium shot to a close-up that contains body parts of only one person even though other characters may be part of the scene being recorded.

Close-Up Shot—Any detail shot where the object of interest being photographed takes up the majority of the frame. Details will be magnified. When photographing a human being, the bottom of frame will just graze the top part of their shoulders and the top edge of frame may just cut off the top part of their head or hair.

Color Temperature—Often referenced on the degrees Kelvin scale, color temperature is a measurement of a light's perceived color when compared to the color of a "perfect black body" exposed to increasing levels of heat. The color temperature for film lighting is generally accepted as around 3200 degrees Kelvin. Sunlight is generally accepted as around 5600 degrees Kelvin. The lower numbers appear warm orange/amber when compared to "white" and the higher numbers appear cool blue.

Composition—In motion picture terms, the artful design employed to place objects of importance within and around the recorded frame.

Continuity—In motion picture production terms: (i) having actors repeat the same script lines in the same way while performing similar physical actions across multiple takes. (ii) Making sure that screen direction is followed from one camera setup to the next. (iii) In postproduction, the matching of physical action across a cut point between two shots of coverage for a scene.

Contrast—The range of dark and light tonalities within a film frame.

Contrast Ratio—The level of delineation between strong areas of dark and strong areas of light within a film frame as represented in a ratio of two numbers. Key + Fill:Fill.

Coverage—Shooting the same action from multiple angles with different framing at each camera setup. Example: A dialogue scene between two people may require a wide, establishing shot of the room, a tighter two-shot of both players, clean singles of each actor, reciprocal over-the-shoulder shots favoring each actor, cutaways of hands moving or the clock on the wall, etc.

Crane—Much like the large, heavy machinery used in construction, a crane on a film set may raise and move camera or have large lighting units mounted to it from high above the set.

Critical Focus—As with the human eye, there can be only one plane or physical slice of reality that is in sharpest focus for the motion picture camera. The plane of critical focus is this slice of space in front of the lens that will show any object within that plane to be in true focus. Example: When recording a person's face in a medium close-up, their eyes should be in sharpest focus. When the eyes are in sharpest focus then the plane of critical focus has been placed at the same distance away from the lens as the actor's eyes.

Cross the Line—Based on the concept inherent to the "action line" or 180 degree rule, this expression refers to accidentally moving the camera across the line and recording coverage for a scene that will not match established screen direction when edited together. See also Jump the Line.

Cutaway—Any shot recorded whose purpose is to allow a break from the main action within a scene. The editor will place a cutaway into an edited scene of shots when a visual break is necessary or when two other shots from the primary coverage will not edit together smoothly.

Daylight Balance—Film and video cameras may be biased toward seeing the color temperature of daylight as "white" light. When they are set this way, they have a daylight balance.

Degrees Kelvin—The scale used to indicate a light source's color temperature, ranging roughly from 1000 to 20,000. Red/orange/amber colored light falls from 1000 to 4000 and bluish light falls from 4500 on up to 20,000.

Depth—The distance from camera receding into the background of the set or location. The illusion of three-dimensional deep space on the two-dimensional film plane.

Depth of Field (DoF)—In filmmaking terms, the DOF refers to a zone, some distance from the camera lens, where any object will appear to be in acceptable focus to the viewing audience. The depth of field lives around the plane of critical focus, but rather than being centered equally, it appears one-third in front of and two-thirds behind the point of critical focus. Any object outside the DOF will appear blurry to the viewer. The DOF may be altered or controlled by changing the camera to subject distance or by adding light to or subtracting light from the subject.

Director of Photography (DP, DOP)—The person on the film's crew who is responsible for the overall look of a motion picture project's recorded image. He or she helps in planning the angles, composition, and movement of the camera as well as design details such as color palettes, textures, and lighting schemes.

Dirty Single—A medium shot to a close-up that contains the main person of interest for the shot but also contains some visible segment of another character who is also part of the same scene. The clean single is made "dirty" by having this sliver of another's body part in the frame.

Dolly—Traditionally, any wheeled device used to move a motion picture camera around a film set either while recording or in between takes. A dolly may be three or four wheeled; ride on the floor or roll (with special wheels) along straight or curved tracks; have a telescoping or booming arm that lifts and lowers the camera.

Domestic Cutoff—The outer 10% of transmitted picture information that is cut off at the outside edges of a cathode ray tube television set and not viewable by the in-home audience. This phenomenon should be taken into account when composing a shot for a project that will be broadcast on television.

Dutch Angle/Dutch Tilt—In filmmaker terms, any shot where the camera is canted or not level with the actual horizon line. The "Dutch angle" is often used to represent a view of objects or actions that are not quite right, underhanded, diabolical, or disquieting. All horizontal lines within the frame go slightly askew diagonally and, as a result, any true vertical lines will tip in the same direction.

End Frame—Any time the camera has been moving to follow action, the camera should come to a stop before the recorded action ceases. This clean, static frame will be used by the editor in order to cut away from the moving shot to any other shot that would come next. Moving frames cut to static frames is a very jarring visual cut and this static end frame helps prevent this mistake.

Establishing Shot—Traditionally the first shot of a new scene in a motion picture. It is a wide shot that reveals the location where the immediately following action will take place. One may quickly learn place, rough time of day, rough time of year, weather conditions, historical era, and so on by seeing this shot.

Exposure—In motion picture camera terms, it is the light needed to create an image on the recording medium (either emulsion film or a video light sensor). If you do not have enough light you will underexpose your image and it will appear too dark. If you have too much light you will overexpose your image and it will appear too bright.

Exterior—In film terms, any shot that has to take place outside.

Eye Light—A light source placed somewhere in front of talent that reflects off the moist and curved surface of the eye. Sometimes called the "life light," this eye twinkle brings out the sparkle in the eye and often informs an audience that the character is alive and vibrant. Absence of the eye light can mean that a character is no longer living or is hiding something, etc.

Eye-Line Match—When shooting clean single coverage for a two person dialogue scene, the eyes of the two characters should be looking off frame in the direction of where the other character's head/face would be. Even though both actors may not be sitting next to one another as they were in the wider two-shot, the eye-line of each "looking" at the other must match from shot to shot so that there is consistency in the edited scene.

Fill Light—A light, of lesser intensity than the key light, used to help control contrast on a set but most often on a person's face. It is "filling" in the shadows caused by the dominant key light.

Film Gauge—In the world of emulsion film motion pictures, the physical width of the plastic film strip is measured in millimeters (i.e., 16 mm, 35 mm). This measurement of film width is also referred to as the film's gauge.

Film Space—The world within the film, both that which is currently presented on screen and that which is "known" to exist within the film's reality.

Fish-Eye Lens—A camera lens whose front optical element is so convex (or bulbous like the eye of a fish) that it can gather light rays from a very wide span. The resulting image formed while using such a lens often shows a distortion in the exaggerated expansion of physical space, object sizes, and perspective.

Focal Length—The angle of view that a particular lens can record. A number, traditionally measured in millimeters (mm), that represents a camera lens' ability to gather and focus light. A lower focal length number (i.e., 10 mm) indicates a wide angle of view. A higher focal length number (i.e., 200 mm) indicates a narrower field of view where objects further from the camera appear to be magnified.

Focus—The state where objects being viewed by the camera appear to be sharply edged, well defined, and show clear detail. Anything out of focus is said to be blurry.

Following Focus—If a subject moves closer to or further away from camera but stays within the film frame, often the camera assistant or camera operator must manually control the focus of the recording lens in order to keep the moving subject in clear, crisp focus. If the subject at the plane of critical focus moves away from that plane and outside the corresponding depth of field, they will get blurry unless the camera assistant follows focus.

Foreground—The zone within a filmed frame that starts near the camera's lens but ends before it reaches a more distant zone where the main action may be occurring. Any object that exists in the foreground of the recorded frame will obscure everything in the more distant zones out to the infinity point.

Foreshortening—In the visual arts, it is a way that three-dimensional objects get represented on the two-dimensional plane. When pictured from a certain view or perspective, the object may appear compressed and/or distorted from its actual shape.

Fourth Wall—In fictional narrative filmmaking, this term means the place from where the camera objectively observes the action on the film set. Since it is possible for the camera to record only three of the four walls within a film set, the fourth wall is the space on set where the camera lives and it is from that privileged place where it observes the action.

Frame—The entire rectangular area of the recorded image with zones of top, bottom, left, right, and center.

Front Lighting—Any lighting scheme where lights come from above and almost directly behind the camera recording the scene. Talent, when facing toward the camera, will have an overall even lighting, which often causes a flatness to their features.

Geared Head—A professional piece of camera support used on dollies, cranes, and tripods that has two spinning geared wheels that allow for very fluid vertical and horizontal movements of the camera. The camera operator must crank each gear wheel manually in order to maintain the appropriate framing.

Gel—Heat-resistant sheet of flexible plastic film that contains a uniform color. Used to add a "wash" of color on a film set. Example: When the feeling of sunset is required for a shot, one can place an orange/yellow gel between the lights and the set to give the impression of a warmer sunset color.

Golden Hour—The moments just after direct sunset but before the ambient light in the sky fades to nighttime darkness. Filmmakers often appreciate the visual quality the soft top light of dusk creates on exterior scenes; sometimes called Magic Hour.

Grip—A film crew member whose job it is to move, place, and tweak any of the various pieces of film equipment used for support of camera and lighting units, or devices used to block light, among other duties. A special dolly grip may be used to rig the dolly tracks and push or pull the dolly/camera during the recording of a shot.

Handheld—Operating the motion picture camera while it is supported in the hands or propped upon the shoulder of the camera operator. The human body acts as the key support device for the camera and is responsible for all movement achieved by the camera during the recording process.

Hard Light—A quality of light defined by the presence of strong, parallel rays being emitted by the light source. Well-defined, dark shadows are created by hard light.

Head—A common film term for the beginning of a shot, especially during the postproduction editing process.

Headroom—The free space at the top of the recorded frame above the head of the talent. Any object may have "headroom." Too much headroom will waste valuable space in the frame and not enough may cause your subject to appear cut off or truncated.

High Angle Shot—Any shot where the camera records the action from a vertical position higher than most objects being recorded. Example: The camera, looking out a third floor window of a house, records a car pulling into the driveway down below.

High Definition (HD)—A reference to the increased image quality and wider frame size (16 × 9) of the more recent digital video format. The increase in line resolution per frame (720 or 1080) increases the sharpness and color intensity of the playback image.

High Key Lighting—A lighting style in which a low contrast ratio exists between the brightly lit areas and the dark areas of the frame. Overall, even lighting gives proper exposure to most of the set and characters within it. There are no real dark shadow regions and no real overly bright regions.

HMI—A film lighting fixture whose internal lamp burns in such a way as to emit light that matches daylight/sunlight in color temperature (5500–6000 degrees Kelvin).

Hood Mount—A device used to mount a tripod head and camera to the hood of a motor vehicle such that the occupants of the vehicle may be recorded while the vehicle is in motion. Often a large suction cup is employed to help secure the camera rig to the hood.

Glossary

Horizon Line—The distant line that cuts across a film frame horizontally. It is used to help establish the scope of the film space and helps define the top and bottom of the film world.

Imaginary Line—The invisible line created by talent sight lines that helps establish what side of the action the camera can record coverage for that scene. The camera should not be moved to the opposite side of this action line because it will cause a reversal in the established screen direction. See also 180 Degree Rule, Sight Line, Axis of Action.

Interior—In film terms, any shot that has to take place inside.

Iris—In motion picture equipment terms, the iris refers to the aperture or flexible opening of the camera lens that controls how much or how little light is used to expose the image inside the camera. Most modern video cameras use an electronic iris that has a thumb wheel, which manually controls the setting for more or less light. Most high end emulsion film and HD lenses use an iris of sliding metal blades that overlap to make the aperture smaller or wider.

Jump Cut—An anomaly of the edited film when two very similar shots of the same subject are cut together and played. A "jump" in space or time appears to have occurred, which often interrupts the viewer's appreciation for the story being shown.

Jump the Line—Based on the concept inherent to the "action line" or 180 degree rule, this expression refers to accidentally moving the camera across the line and recording coverage for a scene that will not match established screen direction when edited together.

Key Light—The main light source around which the remaining lighting plan is built. Traditionally, on film sets, it is the brightest light that helps illuminate and expose the face of the main talent in the shot.

Kicker Light—Any light that hits the talent from a ¾ backside placement. It often rims just one side of the hair, shoulder, or jaw line.

Legs—An alternate name for a camera tripod.

Lens Axis—In motion picture camera terms, it is the central path cutting through the middle of the circular glass found in the camera's taking lens. Light traveling parallel to the lens axis is collected by the lens and brought into the camera exposing the recording medium. One can trace an imaginary straight line out of the camera's lens (like a laser pointer) and have it fall on the subject being recorded. That subject is now placed along the axis of the lens.

Light Meter—A device designed to read and measure the quantity of light falling on a scene or being emitted from it. Often used to help set the level of exposure on the film set and, consequently, the setting on the camera's iris.

Line—The imaginary line that connects a subject's gaze to the object of interest being viewed by that subject. Example: A man, standing in the entry way of an apartment building, looks at the name plate on the door buzzer. The "line" would be traced from the man's eyes to the name plate on the wall. The next shot may be a big close-up of the name plate itself, giving the audience an answer to the question, "what is he looking at?"

Locked Off—The description of a shot where the tripod head pan and tilt controls are locked tight so that there will be no movement of the camera. If there were a need to make adjustments to the frame during shooting, the pan and tilt locks would be loosened slightly for smooth movement.

Long Shot—When photographing a standing human being, their entire body is visible within the frame and a good deal of the surrounding environment is also visible around them. Sometimes called a wide shot.

Look Room/Looking Room/Nose Room—When photographing a person, it is the space between their face and the farthest edge of the film frame. If a person is positioned frame left and is looking across empty space at frame right, then that empty space is considered the look room or nose room.

Low Angle Shot—Any shot where the camera records the action from a vertical position lower than most objects being recorded. Example: The camera, on a city sidewalk, points up to the tenth floor to record two men cleaning the windows.

Low Key Lighting—A lighting style in which a large contrast ratio exists between the brightly lit areas and the dark areas of the frame. Example: Film noir used low key lighting to create deep, dark shadows and single source key lighting for exposure of principal subjects of importance.

Matching Shots (Also Known As Reciprocating Imagery)—When shooting coverage for a scene, each camera setup favoring each character being covered should be very similar if not identical. One should match the framing, camera height, focal length, lighting, and so forth. When edited together, the "matching shots" will balance one another and keep the information presented about each character consistent.

Medium Shot—When photographing a standing human being, the bottom of the frame will cut off the person around the waist.

Middle Ground—The zone within a filmed frame where the majority of the important visual action will take place. Objects in the middle ground may be obscured by other objects in the foreground, but middle ground objects may then also obscure objects far away from camera in the background.

Monocular Vision (Camera Lens)—A visual system in which only one lens takes in and records all data. The three-dimensional aspect of human binocular vision is not present in the monocular vision of the film or video camera.

Motivated Light—Light, seen on a film set, that appears to be coming from some light source within the actual film world.

Natural Light—Any light that is made by the sun or fire; nonman-made sources.

Negative Space—An artistic concept wherein unoccupied or empty space within a composition or arrangement of objects also has mass, weight, importance, and is worth attention.

Neutral Density Filter—A device that reduces the amount of light entering a camera (density), but does not alter the color temperature of that light (neutral). It is either a glass filter that one can apply to the front of the camera lens or, with many video cameras, a setting within the camera's electronics that replicates the reduced light effect of neutral density filters.

Normal Lens—A camera lens whose focal length closely replicates what the field of view and perspective might be on certain objects if these same objects were seen with human eyes.

Objective Shooting—A style of camera operation where the talent never addresses the existence of the camera. The camera is a neutral observer not participating actively in the recorded event but simply acting as a viewer of the event for the benefit of the audience.

Overexposed—A state of an image where the bright regions contain no discernible visual data but appear as glowing white zones. The overall tonality of this image may also be lacking in true "black" values so that everything seems gray to white in luminance.

Overheads—Drawings or diagrams of the film set, as seen from above like a bird's-eye view, that show the placement of camera, lighting equipment, talent, and any set furnishings, etc. These overheads will act as a map for each department to place the necessary equipment in those roughed-out regions of the set.

Overlapping Action—While shooting coverage for a particular scene, certain actions made by talent will have to be repeated from different camera angles and framings. When cutting the film together, the editor will benefit from having the talent making these repeated movements, or overlapping actions, in multiple shots so that when the cut is made it can be made on the matching movement of the action from the two shots.

Over the Shoulder (OTS)—A shot used in filmmaking where the back of a character's head and one of his shoulders occupy the left/bottom or right/bottom foreground and act as a "frame" for the full face of another character standing or seated in the middle ground opposite from the first character. This shot is often used when recording a dialogue scene between two people.

Pan—Short for panorama, the horizontal movement, from left to right or right to left, of the camera while it is recording action. If using a tripod for camera support, the pan is achieved by loosening the pan lock on the tripod head and using the pan handle to swivel the camera around the central pivot point of the tripod in order to follow the action or reveal the recorded environment.

Pan Handle—A tripod head with a horizontal pivot axis allows for the panning action of the camera either left or right. The pan handle is a stick or length of metal tubing that extends off the tripod head and allows the camera operator to control the rate of movement of the camera pan by physically pushing or pulling it around the central axis point of the tripod.

Point of View—In filmmaking terms, any shot that takes on a subjective stance. The camera records exactly what one of the characters is seeing. The camera sits in place of the talent, and what it shows to the viewing audience is supposed to represent what the character is actually seeing.

Point Source—A light source derived from a specific, localized instance of light generation/emission. A nondiffused light source.

Postproduction—The phase of motion picture creation that traditionally happens after all of the live-action film or video is shot (also known as production). Postproduction can include picture and sound editing, title and graphics creation, motion effects rendering, color correction, musical scoring and mixing, etc.

Practical—A functional, onset lighting fixture visible in the recorded shot's frame that may actually help illuminate the set for exposure. Example: A shot of a man sitting down at a desk at night. Upon the desk is a desk lamp whose light illuminates the face of the man.

Preproduction—The period of work on a motion picture project that occurs prior to the start of principal photography (also known as production).

Production—The period of work on a motion picture project that occurs while the scenes are being recorded on film or video. This could be as short as a single day for a commercial or music video or last several months for a feature film.

Proscenium Style—In theatre as well as motion pictures, this is a way to stage the action such that it is seen from only one direction. The audience or, in film's case, the camera views and records the action from only one angle.

Pulling Focus—Camera lenses that have manual controls for the focus will allow a camera assistant or camera operator to move the plane of critical focus closer to the camera, therefore shifting what appears to be in sharp focus within the frame being recorded. This is often done to shift focus from one farther object in the frame to one closer object within the frame.

Pushing Focus—Camera lenses that have manual controls for the focus will allow a camera assistant or camera operator to move the plane of critical focus further away from the camera, therefore shifting what appears to be in sharp focus within the frame being recorded. This is often done to shift focus from a near object in the frame to one further away.

Rack Focus—During the recording of a shot that has a shallow depth of field, the camera assistant or camera operator may need to shift focus from one subject in the frame to another. This shifting of planes of focus from one distance away from the camera to another is called racking focus.

Reveal—Any time that the filmmaker shows new, important, or startling visual information on the screen through camera movement, talent blocking, or edited shots in postproduction. The reveal of information is the payoff after a suspenseful expectation has been established within the story.

Rim Light—Any light source whose rays "rim" or "halo" the edges of a subject or an object on the film set, often set somewhere behind the subject.

Rule of Thirds—A commonly used gauge of film frame composition where an imaginary grid of lines falls across the frame, both vertically and horizontally, at the mark of thirds. Placing objects along these lines or at the cross points of two of these lines is considered part of the tried and true composition of film images.

Safe Action Line—Related to the domestic cutoff phenomenon, the safe action line is found on many camera viewfinders and is used to keep the important action composed more toward the inner region of the frame. This prevents important action from being cut off.

Scene—A segment of a motion picture that takes place at one location. A scene may be composed of many shots from different camera angles or just one shot from one camera setup.

Screen Direction—The direction in which a subject moves across or out of the frame. Example: A person standing at the center of frame suddenly walks out of frame left. The movement to the left is the established screen direction. When the next shot is cut together for the story, the same person must enter the frame from frame right, continuing their journey in the same screen direction—from the right to the left.

Shooting Ratio—The amount of material you shoot for a project compared to the amount of material that makes it into the final edit. Example: You shoot fourteen takes of one actor saying a line, but only use one of those takes in the final movie. You have a 14:1 shooting ratio for that one line of dialogue.

Shot—One action or event that is recorded by one camera at one time. A shot is the smallest building block used to edit a motion picture.

Shot List—A list of shots, usually prepared by the director during preproduction, that acts as a guide for what shots are required for best coverage of a scene in a motion picture project. It should show the shot type and may follow a number and letter naming scheme.

Shot-Reverse-Shot—A term applied to an editing style where one shot of a particular type (medium close-up) is used on one character and then the same type of shot

Glossary

(medium close-up) is edited next to show the other character in the scene. You see the shot, reverse the camera, and see a matching shot of the other.

Side Lighting—A method of applying light to a subject or film set where the lights come from the side, not above or below.

Sight Line—The imaginary line that traces the direction in which a subject is looking on screen; sometimes called a line of attention. Sight line also establishes the line of action and sets up the 180 degree arc for shooting coverage of a scene.

Silhouette—A special way of exposing a shot where the brighter background is correct in its exposure on film but the subject (in the MG or FG) is underexposed and appears as a black shape with no detail but the edge shape.

Slate (noun)—The clapboard used to identify the shot being recorded. Often the name of the production, director, DP, the shooting scene, and the date are written on the slate. (verb)—Using the clapboard sticks to make a "clapping" sound, which serves as a synchronization point of picture and sound tracks during the edit process.

Soft Light—Any light that has diffused, nonparallel rays. Strong shadows are very rare if one uses soft light to illuminate talent.

Spreader (Tripod)—The three legs of a tripod are often attached to a rubber or metal device in order to keep the legs from splaying too far apart while the heavy camera sits atop the tripod head. This three-branched brace allows for greater stability, especially as the tripod legs are spread further and further apart to get the camera lower to the ground.

Staging—The placement of talent and objects within the film set.

Standard Definition—A reference to the normal image quality and frame size of most televisions around the world during the twentieth century. Limitations in broadcast bandwidth, among other technological reasons, required a low resolution image of the 4:3 aspect ratio for television reception in the home.

Start Frame—Any time the camera needs to move in order to follow action, the camera should begin recording, stay stationary for a few moments while the action begins, and then start to move to follow the action. The start frame is required by the editor of the film so that the shot will have a static frame to start on at the beginning of the cut. Static frames cut to moving frames is a very jarring visual cut and this static start frame helps prevent this mistake.

Sticks—(i) An alternate name for a camera tripod. (ii) The clapboard or slate used to mark the synchronicity point of picture and sound being recorded.

Storyboards—Drawings often done during preproduction of a motion picture that represent the best guess of what the ultimate framing and movement of camera shots will be when the film goes into production. These comic book-like illustrations act as a template for the creative team when principal photography begins.

Subjective Shooting—A style of camera operation where the talent addresses the camera straight into the lens (as in news broadcasting) or when the camera records exactly what a character is observing in a fictional narrative as with the point of view shot.

Tail—The common film term for the end of a shot, especially during the postproduction editing process.

Tail Slate—Often used while recording documentary footage, a tail slate is the process of identifying the shot and "clapping" the slate after the action has been recorded but before the camera stops rolling.

Take—Each action, event, or dialogue delivery recorded in a shot may need to be repeated until its technical and creative aspects are done to the satisfaction of the filmmakers. Each time the camera rolls to record this repeated event is a "take." Takes are traditionally numbered starting at "one."

Taking Lens—The active lens on a motion picture or video camera that is actually collecting, focusing, and controlling the light for the recording of the image. On certain models of emulsion film motion picture cameras there can be more than one lens mounted to the camera body. Most video cameras have but one lens, which would be the "taking" lens.

Talking Head—Any medium close-up shot or closer that really just focuses on one person's head and shoulders. Usually associated with documentaries, news, and interview footage.

Three Point Lighting—A basic but widely used lighting method where a key light is employed for main exposure on one side of talent, a fill light to contrast control on the opposite side, and a back light for subject/background separation.

Tilt—The vertical movement, either down up or up down, of the camera while it is recording action. If using a tripod for camera support, the tilt is achieved by loosening

Glossary

the tilt lock on the tripod head and using the pan handle to swing the camera lens up or down in order to follow the vertical action or reveal the recorded environment.

Time Code—A counting scheme based on hours, minutes, seconds, and frames used to keep track of image and sound placement on videotapes.

Tracks/Rail—Much like railroad tracks, these small scale metal rails are used to smoothly roll a dolly across surfaces, either inside or outside, in order to get a moving shot.

Tripod—A three-legged device, often with telescoping legs, used to support and steady the camera for motion picture shooting. The camera attaches to a device capable of vertical and horizontal axis movements called the tripod head, which sits atop the balancing legs.

Truck In/Out—Moving the camera into set or pulling camera out of set, usually atop a dolly on tracks. Also known as tracking in and tracking out.

Tungsten Balanced—Film and video cameras may be biased toward seeing the color temperature of tungsten lamps as "white" light. When they are set this way, they have a tungsten balance.

Two-Shot—Any shot that contains the bodies (or body parts) of two people.

Underexpose—A state of an image where the dark regions contain no discernible visual data but appear as deep black zones. The overall tonality of this image may also be lacking in true "white" values so that everything seems gray down to black in luminance.

Vanishing Point—A long-established technique in the visual arts where opposing diagonal lines converge at the horizon line to indicate the inclusion of a great distance in the image's environment. It is an illusion used to help represent three-dimensional space on a two-dimensional surface.

Video Format—Videotapes record electronic voltage fluctuations or digital bit data that represent picture and sound information. Video cameras are manufactured to record that data onto the tape in a particular way. The shape, amount of data, frame rate, color information, and so forth that gets recorded are determined by the technologies inside the video camera. Examples include NTSC-525 line, PAL, HD-1080i, HD-720p.

Visible Spectrum—The zone in electromagnetic energy waves that appears to our eyes and brains as colored light.

Voice Slate—A practice used at the head of a shot after the camera is rolling and before the director calls "action." Often, a camera assistant will verbally speak the scene and take number so as to identify audio data that may be recorded separately from the picture.

Zoom Lens—A camera lens whose multilens construction and telescoping barrel design allow it to gather light from a wide range or field of view and also from a very narrow (more magnified) field of view. The focal length of the lens is altered by changing the distances of the optical elements contained within the lens barrel itself. Most modern video cameras have built-in optical zoom lenses that can be adjusted from wide to telephoto with the touch of a button.

Index

A

ACT
    definition, 189
    shot matching, 95
Action
    continuity, 140
    definition, 189
    excess overlapping, 141
    loose pan follow-up, 139
    matching speed, 140–141
Angle on Action
    and composition, 33
    definition, 190
Angle of Incidence
    character lighting, 88
    definition, 189
Angle of View
    definition, 190
    zoom shot, 160
Aperture
    definition, 190
    and depth of focus, 72
    and light, 90
    and light quantity, 80
Artificial Light
    definition, 190
    understanding, 186
Aspect Ratio, see also
        Frame Size
    and audience, 5
    basic concept, 6–7
    definition, 190
    history, 7
Atmospherics
    definition, 190
    depth cues, 65
Attention
    definition, 190
    line and screen direction, 100–101
Audience, visual element
        importance, 4–5
Axis of Action
    application, 102–103
    definition, 190

B

Background (BG)
    definition, 190
    depth cues, 65
    film space depth, 64
    focus comparisons, 71, 73
Back Light
    character lighting, 86
    definition, 190
Basic Shots, extended family, 12–20
BCU, see Big Close-Up (BCU)
BG, see Background (BG)
Big Close-Up (BCU)
    characteristics, 19
    example, 13
    shooting, 134
    subject's eyes, 156
    talent movements, 141
Binocular Vision, see also Human Visual System
    definition, 191
    and third dimension, 54–55
Blocking
    definition, 191
    for dynamic shots, 114
    film space depth, 154
Boom Arm
    definition, 191
    dynamic shots, 124
    styles, 125
Bounce Boards, natural vs. artificial light, 78
Bounce Cards, natural vs. artificial light, 78
Break Frame
    definition, 191
    with human subjects, 134
Breaking Rules, 178

C

Camera Angle
    and composition, 32–33
    definition, 191
    and diagonal lines, 61–62
    horizontal, 34–39
    shot matching and dialogue, 148–149
    vertical, 40

Camera Lens
  as composition eye, 66
  definition, 200
  fish-eye, 68–69, 170–171, 195
  focus, 70–71
  normal, 200
  normal vs. zoom, 67–68
  single taking, 55
  taking lens, 205
  very wide angle, 68–69
  wide, CU shots, 170–171
  zoom, 66–69, 160–161, 207
Camera Movement
  cutting, 166
  in dynamic shots, 115
  equipment for, 122
  handheld considerations, 116
  hiding, 169
  pan and tilt shooting, 120
  recording time, 165
Camera Operator
  definition, 191
  eye-line directions, 158–159
  grammar basics, 2
Camera Person
  definition, 191
  grammar basics, 2
Camera Setup
  definition, 191
  grammar basics, 2
Camera Support
  definition, 191
  handheld, 116
Canted Angle, and composition, 59
Character Lighting, three point method, 86–89
Charge-Coupled Device (CCD)
  definition, 191
  DOF control, 172
  natural vs. artificial light, 78
Chiaroscuro
  definition, 191
  understanding, 186
Clean Single, definition, 192
Close-Up Shot (CU)
  characteristics, 8–9, 17–18
  definition, 192
  distracting objects, 153
  example, 13
  headroom, 152
  imaginary line, 103

jumping the line, 104–105
  shot matching and dialogue, 148
  subject's eyes, 156–157
  talent movements, 141
  viewer involvement, 182
  wide lens issues, 170–171
Color
  choices, 151
  set and location lighting, 90
Color Temperature
  and composition, 77
  definition, 192
  video vs. film, 79
Communication, with talent, 132–133
Composition
  basics, 52
  camera angle, 32–33
  camera lens as eye, 66
  character lighting, 86–89
  color temperature, 77
  and contrast, 84–85
  definition, 192
  depth cues, 65
  diagonal lines, 60–62
  direct to camera two-shot, 48–50
  Dutch angle, 59
  film space depth, 63–64
  hard vs. soft light, 82–83
  and headroom, 25, 152
  high angle shot, 41
  horizon line, 56–58
  horizontal camera angle, 34–39
  human subject framing, 24
  lens focus, 70–71
  light as energy, 76
  light factor, 74–75
  light quantity, 80–82
  look room, 28–29
  low angle shot, 42–43
  natural vs. artificial light, 78–79
  over-the-shoulder two-shot, 50–51
  overview, 23
  profile two-shot, 45–47
  pulling vs. following focus, 71–73
  rule of thirds, 30–31
  set and location lighting, 90–91
  subjective vs. objective shooting
    styles, 26–27
  and third dimension, 54–55
  3D space, 53

two-shot, 44
vertical camera angles, 40
zoom lens, 66–69
Compressing, high angle shot, 41
Consistency, in shot matching, 95
Continuity
action, 140
definition, 192
in edit prethinking, 96
screen direction, 97–99
traps, 168
Contrast
and composition, 84–85
definition, 192
Contrast Ratio
character lighting, 86–87
definition, 192
Coverage
definition, 192
in edit prethinking, 96
Crab, dynamic shots, 126
Crane
definition, 192
dynamic shots, 129
Critical Focus
definition, 192–193
focus comparisons, 72
Cross the Line
definition, 193
in edit prethinking, 104–105
CU, see Close-Up Shot (CU)
Cutaway
definition, 193
180 Degree Line crossing, 163

D

Daylight Balance
and composition, 78
definition, 193
Degrees Kelvin
color temperature, 77
definition, 193
Depth
definition, 193
and diagonal lines, 62
film space, 154
foreground, 63
Depth Cues
and composition, 65
fisheye lens, 68–69

Depth of Field (DOF)
control, 72, 172–173
definition, 193
and lens focus, 70
and light quantity, 81
pulling vs. following focus, 71–73
Diagonal Lines, and composition, 60–62
Dialogue, and shot matching, 148–149, 155
Director of Photography (DP, DOP)
definition, 193
viewer and visual elements, 4
Direct to Camera, two-shot, 48–50
Dirty Single, definition, 194
Distance, DOF control, 172
Distractions, removal, 153
Documentary Footage, discretion
during, 167
DOF, see Depth of Field (DOF)
Dolly
crab dolly, 126
definition, 194
dynamic shots, 124, 127–128
motivation, 162
styles, 125
trucking, 127–128
truck in/out definition, 206
Domestic Cutoff
definition, 194
working practices, 138
DOP/DP, see Director of Photography
(DP, DOP)
Dutch Angle
and composition, 59
definition, 194
Dutch Tilt
and composition, 59
definition, 194
Dynamic Shots
blocking talent, 114
camera in motion, 115
camera movement equipment, 122
crab dolly, 126
cranes and jibs, 129
dolly, 124–125
handheld considerations, 116
overview, 113
pan and tilt, 117–121
Steadicam, 128
tripod, 123
truck, 127–128

E

ECU, see Extreme Close-Up (XCU, ECU)
Editor, dialogue and shot matching, 155
Edit prethinking
  continuity, 96
  eye-line match, 111
  imaginary line, 102–103
  line and screen direction, 100–101
  prethinking, 93–94
  reciprocating imagery, 108–110
  screen direction continuity, 97–99
  shooting for, 179
  shooting overlapping action, 140
  shot matching, 95
  30 Degree Rule, 106–107
ELS, see Extreme Long Shot (XLS, ELS)
End Frame
  definition, 194
  pan and tilt, 120–121
Equipment
  for camera movement, 122
  operational knowledge, 184
Establishing Shot
  definition, 194
  Extreme Long Shot, 12
Exposure
  definition, 194
  as light quantity, 80–82
Exterior
  alternate locations, 183
  cranes, 129
  daylight shots, 72, 81
  definition, 194
  depth cues, 65
  depth of field, 172
  extended shot family, 12, 14, 16–19
  golden hour, 196
  horizon line, 56
Extreme Close-Up (XCU, ECU)
  characteristics, 19–20
  example, 13
  focus comparisons, 72
  shooting, 134
Extreme Long Shot (XLS, ELS)
  characteristics, 12–14
  example, 13, 14
  and horizon line, 56
Eye
  lens focus, 70–71
  subject, 156–157

viewer's eye, 150, 181–182
Eye Light
  definition, 194–195
  subject's eyes, 156
  working practices, 136–137
Eye-Line Match
  in closer shots, 158–159
  definition, 195
  edit prethinking, 111
Eye Twinkle
  definition, 194–195
  subject's eyes, 156
  working practices, 136–137

F

FG, see Foreground (FG)
Field of View, hiding camera movement, 169
Fill Light
  character lighting, 86
  definition, 195
Film, color temperatures, 79
Film Gauge
  and audience, 5
  definition, 195
Film Space
  background, 64
  definition, 195
  depth, 154
  foreground, 64
  middle ground, 64
Fish-eye Lens
  close-up shots, 170–171
  definition, 195
  depth cues, 68–69
Focal Length
  definition, 195
  DOF control, 172
  grammar basics, 1–2
  hiding camera movement, 169
  zoom lens, 66–69
Focal Plane, and rack focus, 145
Focus
  definition, 195
  dolly trucking, 128
  importance, 144–145
  lens, 70–71
  pulling vs. following, 71–73
Following Focus
  definition, 195–196
  vs. pulling focus, 71–73

Footage, discretion during, 167
Foreground (FG)
  definition, 196
  film space depth, 63
  focus comparisons, 71, 73
Foreshortening
  definition, 196
  high angle shot, 41
4 : 3
  definition, 189
  safe action line, 138
Fourth Wall
  definition, 196
  screen direction continuity, 97
  subjective vs. objective shooting, 26
Frame
  communication with talent, 133
  cutting camera, 166
  definition, 196
  and diagonal lines, 61–62
  focus importance, 144–145
  and horizon line, 56–57
  human subjects, 24
  lens focus, 70–71
  look room space, 146–147
  object placement, 150
  Rule of Thirds example, 31
  screen direction continuity, 98
  talent blocking, 114
  two-shot composition, 44
  viewer and visual elements, 4
Frame Size, see also Aspect Ratio
  and audience, 5
  film and video, 6
Front Lighting
  character lighting, 88
  definition, 196

G

Geared Head
  definition, 196
  dynamic shots, 123
Gel
  color choices, 151
  definition, 196
Golden Hour
  definition, 196
  lighting considerations, 186
Grammar basics, definition, 1
Grey scale, and composition, 84

Grip
  definition, 196–197
  dynamic shot dollies, 124

H

Handheld
  definition, 197
  in dynamic shots, 116
Hard Light
  definition, 197
  vs. soft, 82–83
Head
  camera recording time, 165
  definition, 197
  dynamic shots, 123
  slating, 174–175
Headroom
  and composition, 25, 152
  definition, 197
  and horizon line, 57
  two people frame composition, 44
Head Shot, see Close-Up Shot (CU)
High Angle Shot
  and composition, 41
  definition, 197
High Definition (HD)
  aspect ratio, 6–7
  definition, 197
High Key Lighting
  definition, 197
  purpose, 84–85
HMI
  definition, 197
  natural vs. artificial light, 78
Hood Mount
  definition, 197
  horizontal camera angles, 35
Horizon Line
  and composition, 56–58
  definition, 198
Horizontal Camera Angles, and
  composition, 34–39
Human Subjects
  breaking frame, 134
  eye light, 136–137
  framing rules, 24
  two-shot frame composition, 44
Human Visual System
  definition, 191
  light quantity, 80

Human Visual System (*continued*)
    pan and tilt, 117–118
    proper focus, 144
    third dimension, 54

I

Imaginary Line
    application, 102–103
    definition, 198
Interior
    alternate locations, 183
    car, 48
    color choices, 151
    definition, 198
    extended shot family, 14, 16–19
    location lighting, 90
    nighttime, 72–73
IRIS, definition, 198

J

Jib, dynamic shots, 129
Jump Cut
    definition, 198
    in edit prethinking, 106
Jump The Line
    definition, 198
    in edit prethinking, 104–105

K

Key Light
    character lighting, 86
    definition, 198
Kicker Light
    character lighting, 89
    definition, 198
Kung-Fu Movies, snap zooms, 160

L

Legs
    definition, 198
    dynamic shots, 123
Lens
    as composition eye, 66
    definition, 200
    fish-eye, 68–69, 170–171, 195
    focus, 70–71
    normal, 200
    normal vs. zoom, 67–68
    single taking, 55

    taking lens, 205
    very wide angle, 68–69
    wide, CU shots, 170–171
    zoom, 66–69, 160–161, 207
Lens Axis
    definition, 198–199
    fill light, 86
    medium close-up, 27
Life Light
    definition, 194–195
    subject's eyes, 156
    working practices, 136–137
Light
    camera lens and composition, 66
    color temperature, 77
    in composition, 74–75
    DOF control, 172
    as energy, 76
    hard vs. soft, 82–83
    natural vs. artificial, 78–79
    sensitivity and exposure, 80–82
    understanding, 186
Light Flares, as problem, 186
Light Meter
    definition, 199
    and light quantity, 80
Line
    definition, 199
    and screen direction, 100–101
Lines of Direction, establishment, 101
Location Lighting, characteristics, 90–91
Locked Off
    definition, 199
    as shot type, 8
Long Shot (LS)
    characteristics, 10–11, 14–15
    definition, 199
    example, 13, 15
    profile two-shot, 45
Look Room
    and composition, 28–29
    definition, 199
    framing for, 146–147
    two people frame composition, 44
Low Angle Shot
    and composition, 42–43
    definition, 199
Low Key Lighting, definition,
    84, 199
LS, see Long Shot (LS)